Aust

rians

University of New Orleans Press

Bundespräsident
Alexander Van der Bellen

Austria and the United States look back at centuries of shared history and experiences.
From the first Salzburgers at the shores of Georgia to the big immigration waves in the early 20 th century –
Austrians have been coming to America.
At the same time, milestones in Austrian modern history are intertwined with the United States,
from colonial times to the 180th anniversary of the formal establishment of bilateral diplomatic relations,
from the catastrophes of the two World Wars through the Cold War until today:
the United States have left their imprint on Austrian life,
ranging from the generous help of the Marshall Plan after World War II
to its many cultural and artistic exports that have been enriching our senses.
Austrians have been grateful to the U.S. for all their good deeds and contributions,
but also for the unlimited opportunities that Austrian immigrants have been looking for over the past centuries.
And those searching for those opportunities have left their mark on the fabric of modern American life,
encompassing all aspects of society – the academics, the entrepreneurs, the artists, the architects,
but also the steel workers and laborers – they all settled in the New World in search of their dreams and ambitions.
And we do honor their achievements, their work, and also their failures,
as we celebrate their humanity – the trait that unites us.
Today, as we look back at the centuries of our shared history, we can take comfort in the friendship
and the excellent relations between our two nations,
and I am pleased by the flourishing contacts at the political, economic, and individual level.
What started in 1734 has blossomed into a friendship today that we can all be proud of.
This volume celebrates this friendship.

A. Van der Bellen

**Austrian
Embassy**
Washington

Botschafter
Wolfgang Waldner

For almost two centuries, Austrian and U.S. diplomats have been nurturing the relationship
between our two countries, establishing and working with networks of contacts to create
opportunities but also to address challenges as they arise. Against this background, we continue
to celebrate this strong transatlantic bond, from the anniversary of the establishment of bilateral
diplomatic relations more than 180 years ago, to the key role the United States played in
establishing and re-establishing the Austrian Republic after the two World Wars.

However, the first contacts between our two countries occurred at the grassroots level via Austrian
immigration to the United States and until this day, immigrants have created an intertwined mesh of ties
between Austria and the United States that forms the backbone of our friendship. Indeed, as Austrians
have been coming to this country since the 1700s, these citizen ambassadors have helped to form this
wonderful nation over the centuries, making their contribution and gaining so much in return.

As Austrian Ambassador to the U.S. I take great pleasure and pride in following their successes and also
cherish the many opportunities to meet fellow Austrians on this side of the Atlantic. After all, having
spent almost two decades serving in three diplomatic postings in Washington, DC and New York City
with my daughters born here as well, I feel a strong personal bond to the United States myself.

The present volume celebrates many of these stories as it chronicles Austrians' journeys to
America through the centuries until today. I am certain that the close friendship that our two
nations enjoy today will continue to foster cooperation and induce people movements across the
Atlantic also in the decades to come.

W. Waldner

Abo
this
boo

The present volume is part of a larger, ongoing investigation dealing with Austrian immigration to the United States against the backdrop of the Austrian-American relationship. This project is primarily digital in nature and represented in this book's companion website, which can be accessed at *www.austriainusa.org.*

We are aware that it is impossible to list and discuss all Austrian-Americans and their individual contributions in printed format, be it in this book, or in one of the accompanying exhibits, and we do not attempt to do so. Rather, this volume includes merely a cross section of the larger subject matter, and we present examples for illustrative purposes.

At the same time, the digital project this book represents is an ongoing and living one that will expand over time. Anyone wishing to make a meaningful contribution, via a story, artifacts, or photographs, is welcome to get in touch via the website.

Acknowle

The authors would like to thank the following individuals and institutions who made this publication possible:

The Embassy of Austria in the United States and Ambassador Wolfgang Waldner, who commissioned this project, have enabled us to engage with the subject matter. In particular, we would like to thank Thorsten Eisingerich, Director of the Austrian Press and Information Service, for overseeing this project for the Embassy, and we are grateful for the help of his colleagues, Julia Aßl and Franziska Riel, who were instrumental in the final editorial process.

We are grateful for a generous grant by the Future Fund of the Republic of Austria for aiding with the printing cost of this volume and thank Anita Dumfahrt, Herwig Hösele, and Kurt Scholz for their untiring efforts in making research and publication funds available to the Austrian scholarly community.

The Austrian National Library and the director of its Picture Archives and Graphics Department, Dr. Hans Petschar, have provided us with very generous access to their holdings, allowing a thorough survey of the visual materials pertaining to this book and the larger project it represents.

edgments

Furthermore, at *uno press* we would like to thank Abram Himelstein and George Kroening Darby with their team for their sterling support; our designer Kevin Stone has done yeoman's work in producing a presentable book, gorgeously illustrated.

We are grateful to Elfi Thiemer at the Presidential Chancellery of Austria, Karin Schmid-Gerlich at the U.S. Embassy in Vienna, Lonnie Johnson and the Austrian Fulbright Commission, Jason Naum at the Botstiber Foundation, the offices of Norbert Bischofberger and Wolfgang Puck, as well as to Markus Schweiger and Claudia Kraif at the Austrian Marshall Plan Foundation for their generous help while preparing this volume.

In addition, Günter Bischof received support from Jonathan Singerton and Hans Petschar; his work on the biographies of Austrian immigrants, highlighted in this publication, was financially supported by the Botstiber Foundation of Media, Pennsylvania. He would like to thank Terry Kline and Siegfried Beer for making the initial grant possible. At the University of New Orleans, Bischof has enjoyed support from Matthew Tarr, Vice President of Research, Kim Long, the Dean of Liberal Arts and Education, Robert Dupont, the Chair of the History Department, and Marc Landry and Gertraud Griessner, the staff of the Austrian Marshall Plan Center for European Studies.

Printed by KOPA, Lithuania

Introduction: Towards the American Century: Austrians in the United States

The Chicago World's Fair of 1893 was a spectacular affair and may well have rung in the "American Century." This was the first time that the New World had ever hosted a world's fair. Secretary of State Elihu Root noted that the fair "led our people out of the wilderness of the commonplace to new ideas of architectural beauty and nobility" (Larson, *Devil in the White City* 374). Chicago constructed an entire neoclassical city that was brightly illuminated at night (see cover photo), which gave the fairgrounds the name "White City." Chicago's World Columbian Exposition aimed at outdoing the Paris *Exposition Universelle* of 1889 with more attractions and more visitors. The signature Ferris Wheel in Chicago competed with the Eiffel Tower, the symbol of the Paris World's Fair. Representing the U.S. as the brash, new industrial power, Chicago was determined to top the French and to "out-Eiffel Eiffel" (Larson 15). While the Paris World's Fair attracted almost 6.5 million visitors (with a one-day record of 390,000), Chicago attracted 27.5 million visitors (with more than 700,000 people coming on its best day). The success of the Chicago World's Fair put the United States on the map as the premier industrial power in the world, at the same time showing that the nation was also capable of constructing beautiful objects. The fair suggested such a "sense of amplitude and splendor" — a Chicago poet called it "an inexhaustible dream of beauty" (Larson 252) — that the European powers were forced to recognize the United States as a "civilized" nation. More than any other event in transatlantic relations, the Chicago World's Fair signaled the new trend in global affairs towards the American Century.

At a hearing to confirm him as President Reagan's Ambassador to Vienna (1988-90), Henry Grunwald had initially planned to say that Austria was "an important unimportant country," but then he thought better of it (Grunwald 590). Yet, the comment he cut from his speech might be an accurate characterization of Austria's place on the list of hierarchies for U.S. foreign policy today. After the end of the Cold War, Austria no longer held the importance that it enjoyed when it served as East-West mediator and meeting place, as "an unofficial headquarters for the Cold War" (Grunwald 597). Austrians always liked to see themselves as "the small world in which the large world held its rehearsals" ("*die kleine Welt, in der die grosse ihre Probe hält*" - Christian Friedrich Hebbel). Austria-Hungary was a key player at the start of World War I, and the *Anschluss* of "little Austria" in March 1938 was a milestone on the road to World War II. The Habsburg Empire was an important player during the founding of the United States, a new nation starting its ascendancy on the periphery of global political power, which, at the time, was dominated by European nations. However, as the U.S. rose to world-power status in the late 19th century, the Austro-Hungarian Monarchy declined. President Wilson played a principal role in the break-up of the Habsburg Monarchy in 1918/19 at a time when the U.S. had become a key factor in the global power balance: The U.S. had successfully moved from the periphery to the center. Small Republican Austria, politically torn asunder by civil war and economically insignificant, had become a bit player in the world – an "important unimportant" place.

After the U.S. had played a crucial role in the defeat of Hitler's Germany and the Japanese militarists, the American public came to accept the nation's new-found role in the world. In a celebrated article, Henry Luce of *Time* and *Life* magazines asked Americans to embrace their dominant role in the world. After World War II, the U.S. played a crucial role in the world and became the global "police force," regularly intervening in many crisis spots during the Cold War. After the end of the Cold War, the U.S. was the sole superpower ("hyperpower") in the 1990s. But the attacks of 9/11 and the subsequent wars in Iraq and Afghanistan brought about a slow decline that was accelerated by the collapse of Lehman Brothers in 2008 and the financial crisis that followed in its wake. Today, the U.S. is no longer prepared to play the world's "policeman," refusing to fully engage in crisis spots like Syria to maintain regional stability. In the meantime, Austria has been a member of the European Union since 1995; its role in the world has been absorbed in EU foreign policy. It no longer figures as an "important unimportant" place.

This book—and the digital and physical exhibits it accompanies—attempts to tell the story of Austrian immigrants to the United States against the backdrop of the larger trajectory of Austrian-American relations. The first "Austrian" immigrant community was established in Ebenezer, Georgia, in 1734. To be accurate, these "Austrians" hailed from the Archbishopric of Salzburg, so technically they were Salzburgers, expelled being Protestants. In fact, most of them were "German" miners that came to Salzburg in the 16th and 17th century to work in the Alpine gold and silver mines. While most of the expelled Protestants went to Prussia, a small group came to Georgia. "Austrian" immigrants in the 19th century hailed from all parts of the Habsburg Monarchy. In fact, during the early part of the 20th century, prior to World War I, migrants from the Austro-Hungarian Monarchy constituted the largest cohort of immigrants, coming to the United States, looking for work and a better life. Each chapter in this book features immigrants that were typical of their time.

Before and after World War I, people from the Burgenland (a part of Western Hungary that became Austrian after the war) constituted the largest group of "Austrian" immigrants to the U.S., with Fred Astaire as their most prominent representative. As a result of the Dollfuss-Schuschnigg regime and then the *Anschluss* of Austria to the Third Reich in 1938, Vienna's large Jewish community was forced to leave. About 30,000 of them found a haven in the U.S., as did many socialists who were persecuted by the Austro-fascist regime. After World War II, some 5,000 Austrian women moved to the U.S. after they married American occupation soldiers. Many Austrian ski champions came as ski instructors and often became entrepreneurs, building hotels and starting ski resorts. In addition, chefs like Wolfgang Puck and scientists like Norbert Bischofberger came for better economic and educational/professional opportunities, and many stayed and founded thriving companies. Art historian Max Hollein started out at the Guggenheim Museum in New York City and is now the director of the Metropolitan Museum. The former Governor of California Arnold Schwarzenegger and two-time Oscar-winner Christoph Waltz have careers in Hollywood, and they are not the only ones. Since World War I, numerous Austrian film makers such as Billy Wilder and actors like Hedy Lamarr have had tremendous success in Hollywood. The grandchildren of Austrian immigrants, known as "quiet invaders," have also had impressive careers: Galician Jewish immigrant Jonas Bernanke came to the U.S. in the later nineteenth century; his grandson Ben Bernanke became a well-known Princeton economist and the chairman of the Federal Reserve Board (2006-14). The 54th governor of New York (2006-8) Eliot L. Spitzer's paternal grandparents were Galician Jews from the Habsburg Monarchy who settled in the Lower Eastside.

There is no authoritative master narrative of the Austrian-American relationship, which makes it a favorite topic for amateur historians of diplomatic relations. E. Wilder Spaulding, a former American cultural diplomat in Vienna, gives a good overview of Austrian immigration in his book *The Quiet Invaders* (1968). Heinrich Drimmel, a former long-term minister of education, provides a highly biased, at times anti-American survey of 19th century political relations in *Die Antipoden* (1984). Diplomat Erwin Matsch's *Wien–Washington* (1990), a self-proclaimed "journal of diplomatic relations" from its beginnings in 1838 to World War I, presents a selection of diplomatic dispatches defining Austro-American relations.

More recently, eminent historians have supplemented these accounts with their painstaking research and sharp analyses. James Van Horn Melton's *Religion, Community and Slavery on the Colonial Southern Frontier* (2015) is as fine a case study we will ever get of an "Austrian" immigrant cohort in the U.S. It pays equal attention to the "Salzburger's" background and covert religious practices in the Salzburg Alpine valleys and their difficult beginnings in the frontier community of Ebenezer, Georgia. For the crucial period of the American Revolution, Jonathan Singerton's recent University of Edinburgh dissertation "Empires on the Edge: The Habsburg Monarchy and the American Revolution, 1763-1789" (2018) is unmatched in its granular detail and keen analysis. Nicole Phelps's *U.S.-Habsburg Relations from 1815 to the Paris Peace Conference* (2013), her published and revised University of Minnesota dissertation, looks at the bilateral relationship from the perspective of both diplomatic and consular relations. Her work documents and analyzes the process by which the U.S. defined its place in the European political power system during the "long" 19th century. In their highly analytical study *From a Multiethnic Empire to a Nation of Nations* (2017), Annemarie Steidl, Wladimir Fischer Nebmaier, and James W. Oberly focus on the immigration of "Austrians" from all parts of the Habsburg Monarchy.

The three authors analyze census and immigration records from both sides of the Atlantic and paint a rich quantitative picture of immigration from the Habsburg Monarchy that includes the formation of ethnic communities in American cities, the role of so-called "identity managers" in the assimilation process of these migrants, the practice of sending remittances to their home countries, and the Austrians' frequent return migrations. The authors discuss the immigrants' marriage behavior as an important indicator of the speed with which they assimilated. Tara Zahra's *The Great Departure* (2016) focuses on Eastern European mass migration from the 19th to the 20th century and adds additional depth to the discussion of Austrian immigration to the U.S. as does Martin Pollak's *Kaiser von Amerika: Die grosse Flucht aus Galizien* (2010).

There are no 20th century surveys on U.S.-Austrian Relations. A survey by the U.S. Embassy in Vienna, published on the occasion of *175 Years of U.S.-Austrian Diplomatic Relations from 1838 to 2013* (2013), a handsome and richly illustrated volume, is a good start. Günter Bischof's *Relationships/Beziehungsgeschichten* (2014), a collection of essays, provides the closest thing to a survey of Austrian immigration to the U.S. Bischof's *Quiet Invaders Revisited* (2017), an edited collection of immigration biographies, tries to shift the focus in migration studies from statistics and cohorts to individual lives. There are some fine monographic studies on individual periods in Austrian-American relations: Phelps's final two chapters deal with President Woodrow Wilson's policies regarding Austria-Hungary in World War II and his role in breaking up the Habsburg Empire, but Kurt Bednar's *Der Papierkrieg zwischen Washington und Wien 1917/18* (2017) covers the same period in much greater detail. Christian Fleck's *Etablierung in der Fremde* (2015) investigates the difficult process of assimilation/acculturation of well-known Jewish scholars expelled from Austria after the Anschluss. Robert Keyserlingk's *Austria in World War II* (1988) has become a classic. Florian Traussnig's *Militärischer Widerstand von Aussen* (2016) covers the role of Austrian émigrés in the U.S. during World War II, who volunteered and served in the U.S. Army and the Office of Strategic Services, an intelligence service.

For the postwar period, the decade of the Austrian occupation and the crucial role the U.S. played in the re-establishment of Austria, and the country's place in the Cold War, has caught the attention of several researchers: Günter Bischof (*Austria in the First Cold War, 1945-1955,* 1999), Oliver Rathkolb (*Washington Ruft Wien,* 1997*)*, and Reinhold Wagnleitner (*Coca-Colonization and the Cold War,* 1994). Günter Bischof's and Hans Petschar's *The Marshall Plan since 1947* (2017) deals with the role the U.S. played in the reconstruction of the Austrian economy after World War II. Various essays in the journal *Contemporary Austrian Studies* (1994 to Present) deal with aspects of U.S.–Austrian relations during this period. Individual autobiographical writings like Henry Grunwald's *One Man's America* (1997), Frederic Morton's *Runaway Waltz: A Memoir from Vienna to New York* (2005), and Ruth Klüger's *Still Alive* (1992) provide particularly vibrant pictures of Austrian Jewish emigrants and their spectacular careers in the U.S. Margit Reiter's and Helga Embacher's co-edited *Europa und der 11. September 2011* (2011) is a very useful collection of essays on European (including Austrian) responses to the 9/11 terrorist attacks on the U.S.

Our book here presents a survey of Austrian-American relations that goes beyond the 180-year period of official diplomatic relations (1838-2018). Because individual people have shaped the connection between the two countries, this book provides both the 300-year story of Austrian immigration to the U.S. and short profiles of immigrants' lives. It does not, however, look at this bilateral relationship evenly from both sides; the story of Americans in Austria is not part of this book

or the exhibition and the digital project it accompanies. This book, then, is the quasi-catalogue for an exhibit commissioned by the Austrian Embassy in Washington, DC. Ambassador Wolfgang Waldner first presented the idea of commemorating the stories of Austrian-Americans with an exhibit and an accompanying monograph in 2018, both of them designed to look at the Austrian–American relationship in its historical context. Out of this undertaking grew a larger, digital project chronicling this relationship in greater detail via additional multimedia content. With his long service as an Austrian diplomat in the United States—first as Director of the Austrian Cultural Fora in New York and Washington and then as Ambassador to the U.S. since 2016—Waldner has officially represented the bilateral relationship for some twenty years. He commissioned Günter Bischof, long-term scholar of U.S.–Austrian relations and director of the Austrian Marshall Plan Center for European Studies at the University of New Orleans, to work on this project in tandem with Thorsten Eisingerich and Hannes Richter, Waldner's key staffers in the Austrian Press and Information Service, the Embassy's public diplomacy section.

The division of labor was established early on: Bischof would write the text for the exhibit panels and the six book chapters, and maintain academic oversight of the project, while Eisingerich oversaw the editorial process and Richter would focus on illustration and photographic research and establish the digital repository that serves as the nucleus of this ongoing work. With the present volume, we hope to make a contribution to the understanding of Austrians in the United States among the public, while we strive to build the premier digital presence for the subject matter at www.austriainusa.org.

Günter Bischof
Hannes Richter

New Orleans - Washington, DC, April 2019

**Dedicated to
Austrian-Americans,
1734 - today**

Towards the American Century: Austrians in the United States

Günter Bischof - Hannes Richter

Chapter 1

The Beginnings of Austrians in America, 1732-1860

After the Spanish Habsburgs conquered a good part of the New World and, in the course of the 16th century, expanded into the Southeast and Southwest of today's United States, Austrian immigrants followed. In Latin America and the Caribbean, the local authorities usually documented them as "Aleman" (German) and translated their first names into Spanish. For example, the documents almost always list Hans Seisenhoffer, a captain working for the Welser Company, as Juan Aleman. According to Spencer Tye, "'German' master miners came to the Americas under the command of the Welsers. While the Welsers and the Fuggers, the famous Augsburg trading families, certainly favored South German talent when staffing their offices across Europe and the Americas, they often sought out specialists from outside that region. The Welsers recruited heavily from mining towns in Tyrol, Silesia, and further East" (Personal e-mail to author, August 2, 2018). It is quite likely that miners from the Tyrol were the first Austrians to come to the New World, but so far nobody has been able to document them as individuals.

Bartholomeus V. Welser (1484 – 1561) was head of the German bank Welser Brothers, whose enterprises eventually controlled large sectors of the European economy and was instrumental in German colonization of the Americas. It is highly probable that the first Austrians who set foot on American soil were miners from the Tyrol working for Welser enterprises in the New World. However, as of today no documentation of such individuals is available.

Bartholomeus V. Welser's niece, Philippine Welser (1527 – 1580), connected the Welser dynasty with the Austrian House of Habsburg; she married Ferdinand II, Archduke of Austria.

THE "SALZBURGERS" IN EBENEZER, GEORGIA, 1734-

In 1732, Firmian, the Archbishop of Salzburg, expelled some 16,000 Protestants from his Pongau district who had been practicing their religion clandestinely for a couple of centuries. At the time, the Archbishopric of Salzburg was one of some 3,000 semi-autonomous provinces of the Holy Roman Empire until it became part of the Habsburg lands in 1803 and, in 1918, a state of Austria. Jesuit "missionaries" had visited these districts in the early 1730s to investigate "crypto-Protestant" conventicles. According to James Van Horn Melton, the Jesuits reported to the Archbishop that the Gastein valley had served as "a breeding ground for heresy in Salzburg" for a long time (Melton 23). After their expulsion, a group of 38 Gastein miners and peasants emigrated to Southern Germany and then on to the new British colony of Georgia, where, in 1734, they founded Ebenezer, the first Austrian community in the American colonies, north of Savannah. Two more groups of Salzburgers followed. While scholars have traditionally attributed the Salzburgers' move to Georgia to their desire for religious freedom, Melton argues that the miners in the first group were motivated more by the promise of adventure and risk-taking (Melton 113-120). Equipped with "spatial and psychological mobility," they accepted "the perils of migrating to an utterly foreign destination" (Melton 120).

Altogether about 150 Salzburgers settled in Georgia while some 16,000 went to East Prussia. As part of their sponsorship, the Pietist "Francke Foundations" of Halle in Prussia and the "Society for the Promotion of Christian Knowledge" in London sent two pastors along with them to Georgia. Pastor Johann Martin Boltzius, the spiritual leader of the new Ebenezer community, interpreted his congregation's move to Georgia in biblical terms, as an exodus of an exceptional group of Pietists seeking salvation in the frontier wilderness. James Edward Oglethorpe, a member of the British parliament, convinced his government to sponsor the Salzburgers' Georgia expedition. Like Roman soldiers turned farmers and defenders of the Roman Empire, they received 50 acres of land on the Georgia frontier and were expected to defend this British outpost against French and Spanish colonial rivals, as well as Native Americans. For the first two decades of its existence, the colony of Georgia was unique among Southern colonies as it expressly prohibited slavery under the assumption that free men would be less prone to rebellion and defend the British southeastern frontier better than a small elite of slave-holding planters would (Melton 109).

The Salzburgers had a rough start in their new home. After their first allotment of remote land had proven to be too sandy and infertile, Ebenezer needed to be resettled on fertile soil. During the first two years of the "seasoning period [...] conditions and morale were abysmal" (Melton 154). Eighteen of the initial group of 38 Salzburgers perished from dysentery and malaria in swampy, mosquito-ridden coastal Georgia. Pastor Boltzius played a crucial role in keeping them together throughout the ordeal, thanks to his stern spiritual regime and his community-building measures. Replenished by new arrivals and having moved to more fertile land, they managed to survive on subsistence farming and prospered by building corn and lumber mills; the women grew silk.

A member of the Ebenezer community, Johann Adam Treutlen, who came as an indentured servant from the Palatinate, was elected to Georgia's first Commons House in 1764. As a leading supporter of American independence in the Georgia colony, he became the first governor of Georgia in 1777. During the American Revolution, Ebenezer was occupied by rebels and royalists in turn and declined as a result of wide-spread destruction. A trickle of Austrian migrants to the U.S. probably continued throughout the colonial period but they have not been documented.

On the way A hand-colored engraving shows the Salzburger Lutherans leaving their homeland on their way to Georgia in 1732.

Johann Martin Boltzius
Originally created on December 31, 1753, this image
shows Johann Martin Boltzius (1703 – 1765), the
Lutheran minister and administrator of Ebenezer.

Philip Georg Friedrich von Reck traveled with the Salzburgers to Georgia and documented their way to and in the New World. In this drawing, called "The Needles," he depicted two ships, the *Simonds* and the *London Merchant* passing by the Isle of Wright on their way to Georgia in 1735. The Needles, three large chalk cliffs, can be seen in the background.

War Dance Another drawing by von Reck depicts "An Indian War Dance" performed by the Yuchi people during an annual festival. The *Yuchi*, a native American tribe, originally lived in the Tennessee River Valley and later moved to Alabama, Georgia and South Carolina – making them neighbors of the Georgia Salzburgers. According to his notes, von Reck attended such an annual festival twice.

Passenger List of the *Purrysburg*

Philipp Georg Friedrich von Reck, Hanoverian commissioner
Christian Schweikert, servant of von Reck
Johann Martin Boltzius, pastor
Christian Israel Gronau, pastorial assistant
Christopher Ortman, schoolmaster
Juliana Ortmann (wife of Christopher)
Johan Andreas Zwiffler, apothecary

Emigrants	Domicile	Occupation (male)	Year of Death
Gilbert Beque	France	Baker	After 1738
Matthias Braunberger	Bavaria	Miller's helper	1734
Balthasar Fleiss	Gastein	Miner	1734
Thomas Geschwandel	Gastein	Miner	1761
Margaretha Hofer	Gastein	Wife of Thomas	1735
- Margaretha	Gastein	Daughter	1752
Hans Gruber	Gastein	Peasant	1734
Peter Gruber	Gastein	Peasant	1740
Martin Herzog	Pinzgau	Miller	After 1750
Maria Hierl	Liechtenberg	Unmarried maidservant	Unknown
Anna Hofer	Gastein	Unmarried maidservant	1735
Lorenz Huber	Gastein	Miner	1734
Maria Mandelleitner	Gastein	Wife of Lorenz	1734
- Johann	Gastein	Son	1735
- Maria	Gastein	Daughter	1735
- Margaretha		Daughter	After 1752
Tobias Lackner	Gastein	Miner	1734
Christian Leimberger	Leogang	Unmarried manservant	1763
Matthias Mittersteiner	Goldegg	Unmarried manservant	1734
Johann Mosshammer	Zell	Manservant	1735
Maria Kroehr	Saalfelden	Wife of Johann	After 1758
Catharina Piedler	Saalfelden	Unmarried maidservant	After 1750
Leonhard Rauner	Bavaria	Unmarried day laborer	1740
Simon Rauschgot	Goldegg	Unmarried manservant	1735
Simon Reiter	Gastein	Unmarried manservant	After 1757
Maria Reiter	Liechtenberg	Unmarried maidservant	1734
Barbara Rohrmoser	Saalfelden	Peasant (left husband in Salzburg)	1735
- Catharina (Kroehr)	Saalfelden	Daughter	After 1776
- Gertraud (Kroehr)	Saalfelden	Daughter	After 1765
Georg Roth	Würzburg	Distiller	1735
Maria Barbara Oswald	Würzburg	Wife of Georg	After 1736
Georg Schweiger	Gastein	Unmarried manservant	After 1772
Paul Schweighofer	Mittersill	Weaver	1736
Margaretha Priedlinger	Mittersill	Wife of Paul	After 1752
- Maria	Mittersill	Daughter	After 1741
- Thomas	Mittersill	Son	1772
- Ursula	Mittersill	Daughter	Unknown
Christian Steiner	Gastein	Miner	1735

+ 30 English colonists (unlisted)

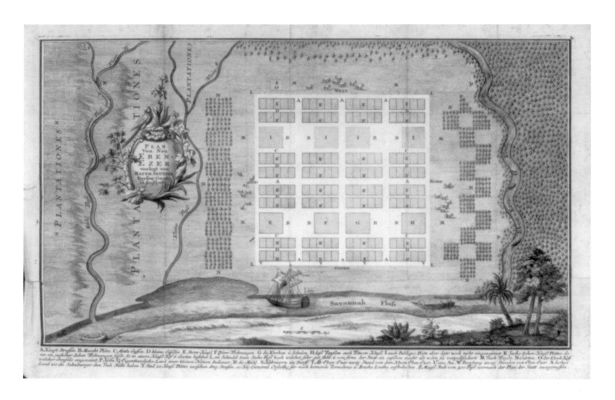

New Ebenezer, Ga. An early plan of the settlement (1742).

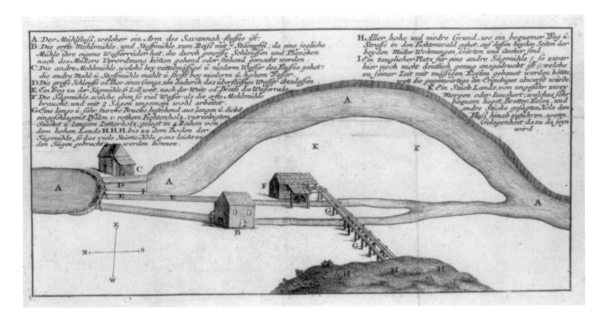

Another depiction of New Ebenezer, Georgia, 1742.

Jerusalem Lutheran Church in Ebenezer, Effingham County, Georgia Completed in 1769, it is the oldest continuous worshipping Lutheran Church in America and among the oldest structures in the state of Georgia.

Interior view of Jerusalem Church, Ebenezer, Georgia.

THE HABSBURGS AND THE AMERICAN WAR OF INDEPENDENCE AND THE ERA OF NON-RECOGNITION, 1776-1838

Even though the citizens of the Habsburg Empire were greatly interested in the American Revolution (1776-1783) and fascinated with Benjamin Franklin, Emperor Joseph II never fully recognized the United States after their hard-earned victory in the bloody war against Great Britain and King George III. In 1778, the Continental Congress dispatched William Lee to Vienna to negotiate the new republic's recognition and establish diplomatic relations. Yet the Imperial Court in Vienna, led by State Chancellor Prince Kaunitz, never granted Lee a formal audience with the Emperor. The court did not want to negotiate with anti-dynastic revolutionaries and upset British royalty. After the Peace Treaty of Paris (1783), Congress gave its representatives in Europe the green light to negotiate a Treaty of Amity and Friendship with the Habsburg Empire. However, Thomas Jefferson, the new U.S. minister in Paris, was not interested in initiating diplomatic relations with the Habsburg Empire and the "whimsical" Emperor Joseph II and used dilatory tactics to postpone negotiations. No treaty was ever signed, and the Habsburg monarchs did not show any "diplomatic interest" in the U.S. republic until 1838.

However, people throughout the Habsburg Monarchy were very interested in the American Revolution. Daily newspapers like the *Wienerische Diarium* (founded in 1703, the oldest newspaper in the world) regularly reported about the events unfolding in the course of the American War of Independence. As long as their publications did not question the authority of the monarchy, newspaper editors were able to maneuver around censorship. Even Jefferson's Declaration of Independence was eventually published; however, the papers did not print the list of grievances against King George III. Even though some were censored, books about the American Revolution reached audiences in

the Habsburg Monarchy. Jonathan Singerton analyzed the correspondence between subjects of the Habsburg Monarchy and Benjamin Franklin, who received 177 letters from Austrian admirers in his Paris domicile (Singerton, Empires on the Edge, Ch. 1). One third of this correspondence was with Dr. Jan Ingenhousz, a Dutch-born physician and scientist who became Empress Maria Theresia's court physician and who delivered news of the American Revolution to the highest levels of the Habsburg court, including the emperor. The Ingenhousz-Franklin correspondence established a link between the Habsburg lands and the New World. News of the American Revolution also reached the Anglophone salons of Vienna.

During the War of Independence, Austrian merchants from Ostende and Trieste lobbied Vienna to negotiate a trade treaty with the British colonies in America. Under the neutral Austrian flag, merchants from the Austrian Netherlands exported weapons, munitions, and gun powder to the American revolutionaries. Trading interests on the periphery of the Habsburg Empire eventually trumped diplomatic caution, and the Austrian Netherlands dispatched Baron Frederick Eugene de Beelen-Bertholff as the first Austrian trade commissioner (the unaccredited "Imperial Commercial Advisor" from 1882-85) to Philadelphia. According to Jonathan Singerton, Prince Kaunitz was reluctant to send him and refused to accredit him, wanting "to see what the fate of the colonies will be" (*Empires on the Edge*, Ch. 5). Trade commissioner Beelen-Bertholff quickly established himself as a premier foreign diplomat in the U.S. capital Philadelphia and sent back valuable reports about trading opportunities in the colonies (including with native Americans such as the Oneida tribe of upstate New York). He also reported on the American national and regional political scene of the mid-1780s. After the Declaration of Independence, the merchants of Trieste established profitable trade connections with the U.S., importing American tobacco and exporting

Monticello - home of Thomas Jefferson in Charlottesville, Virginia (between 1800 and 1906). The glass for the home's dome was imported from Bohemia via Trieste, an example of the rich trade links established between the Habsburg Empire and the United States after gaining their independence.

The Americans did not find it easy to deal with the emperor's chancellor Prince Klemens Metternich, who, to them, embodied reactionary Catholic Austria and its opposition to liberal revolutions and free trade.

cloth, Styrian iron products, and Bohemian glass wares (Jefferson's glass dome at Monticello is made from imported Bohemian glass). No trade treaty was ever signed, yet the entire Monarchy benefited from Beelen-Bertholff's trade relations, not only the Netherlands and Trieste. His regular reports to Vienna and Brussels, according to Singerton, made the Habsburg Monarchy "the most well-informed European power" on economic and political developments in the U.S.

MONARCHICAL HABSBURG AND REPUBLICAN AMERICA: DIPLOMATIC RELATIONS ESTABLISHED (1838-1867)

According to Nicole Phelps, the U.S. and Austria were equally slow to develop diplomatic relations (Phelps 41). Washington sent the first U.S. consul to the busy Habsburg port of Trieste in 1800, but without a clearly defined diplomatic rank, he achieved very little with the court in Vienna. In 1829, the U.S. negotiated its first treaty of commerce and navigation with the Habsburg Empire. It came into force in 1831 and "served as the first instance of official mutual recognition between the U.S. and Habsburg governments" (Phelps 43). The first U.S. consul in Vienna, sent there in 1830, lobbied the government for freer trade policies. In the 1830s, the State Department sent "special tobacco agents" overseas to investigate potential markets for the tobacco-producing Southern states. The Americans did not find it easy to deal with the emperor's chancellor Prince Klemens Metternich, who, to them, embodied reactionary Catholic Austria and its opposition to liberal revolutions and free trade (Phelps 44).

In 1820, Prince Metternich appointed Alois Baron Lederer as the first consul general in New York with Vice-Consulates to follow in New Orleans (1837), Boston, and Philadelphia (1841). In 1829, the two powers signed their first Treaty of Navigation and Commerce. Finally in 1838, fifty years after the first attempt, the Austrian Empire and the U.S. posted ministers and established diplomatic relations: Henry A. Muhlenberg in Vienna (who was soon replaced by a series of short-lived ministers) and Wenzel Mareschal in Washington. Mareschal's assistant, Georg von Hülsemann, a German from Hannover, replaced him as *chargé d'affaires* in 1841 and remained in the U.S. capital until 1863.

Hülsemann represented the Austrian Empire through the stormy period of the 1848/49 revolution, when Hungary declared its independence from the Empire. Vienna almost abandoned relations with the U.S. over Secretary of State Daniel Webster's quasi-support of Hungarian independence and the warm welcome of the revolutionary leader Lajos Kossuth in the U.S., where public opinion was anti-Catholic and anti-Habsburg and pro-Hungarian. While a U.S. Senator proclaimed that Austria "was least of all other powers to be regarded by us," Hülsemann predicted early on that "the adventurous spirit of this country will lead to trouble with everyone."

Prince Klemens Metternich,
the Austrian Emperor's Chancellor.

HENRY A. MUHLENBERG.

Henry A. Muhlenberg, American politician and diplomat, first United States Minister to the Austrian Empire, 1838.

Alois Baron von Lederer, Austrian Consul General in New York, appointed in 1820.

The former Moravian priest Karl Postl was one of them. He left in the late 1820s and adopted the pen name of Charles Sealsfield. He became a prolific Romantic novelist and journalist, penning the anti-Habsburg tract *Austria As It Is* before he retired in Switzerland.

Adventurous Austrians — like the Salzburgers — had emigrated to the U.S. since the days of British colonialism. Between 1821 and 1840, Austrian statistics counted 21,791 persons who left the Monarchy for the U.S. (Steidl et al. 114). The former Moravian priest Karl Postl was one of them. He left in the late 1820s and adopted the pen name of Charles Sealsfield. He became a prolific Romantic novelist and journalist, penning the anti-Habsburg tract *Austria As It Is* before he retired in Switzerland. Nikolaus Lenau from Bukovina came to the U.S. in the early 1830s— only to return as a disappointed man after a rough year of farming on the Ohio frontier. Ferdinand Kürnberger recounted Lenau's experience in his popular americanophobic novel *Der Amerika-Müde* (1855). Austrians also fell victim to "gold fever" after gold was discovered in the American

River outside of Sacramento, California. In 1851, as Thomas Albrich tells the story, Joseph Steinberger from Kitzbühel, along with three Tyrolean friends, traveled more than 200 days that led them from Bremen around Cape Horn to the Golden State. Upon their arrival in San Francisco in 1852, they broke up and went prospecting in Sacramento and Stockton. None struck it rich. Steinberger exhausted himself and died in San Francisco from tuberculosis in 1853. One of them later returned to the Tyrol (*Goldjäger aus Tirol*).

The eminent historian J. Lothrop Motley represented the U.S. in Vienna during the Civil War to protect American interests in Latin America as defined by the Monroe Doctrine. The U.S. resisted Napoleon III's scheme to establish the Habsburg Archduke Maximilian (Emperor Francis Joseph's younger brother) as emperor of Mexico in 1864 during a time of political turmoil. The U.S. never recognized Maximilian but supported the republican government. After the Civil War, Motley opposed sending Austrian volunteers to Mexico to save Maximilian (Phelps 68-75). Despite his protest, 7,000 volunteers from Austria and Belgium (Maximilian's wife Charlotte was King Leopold's only daughter) and 200 officers traveled to Mexico in 1864. Organized as the 2nd Mexican Territorial Division and commanded by General Count Franz Thun-Hohenstein, they constituted a separate unit but operated as a part of the Imperial Mexican armed forces, which served under French command. After the end of the American Civil War, the Americans supported the Republican forces in Mexico against the European intervention. Yielding to American pressure, the French withdrew late in 1866, and 3,500 Austrian volunteers returned home. The rest returned a year later, after Maximilian's capture and execution at Querétaro in 1867, which marked the end of the European intervention.

Charles Sealsfield The Austrian-American journalist Karl Anton Postl, who worked under the pseudonym Chares Sealsfield spent several years in the United States between 1823 and 1858, eventually becoming a U.S. citizen. Born im Moravia, Postl was also a priest and first came to New Orleans via Switzerland in 1832.

Nikolaus Lenau Drawn by fantasies about American life, the writer Nikolaus Lenau came to the United States in 1832. He bought land in Ohio, but did not devote much attention to it. Dissapointed by life in America, he returned to Austria in 1833.

Thomas Geschwandel (1693-1761)

Thomas Geschwandel was a miner from the Gastein Valley, who came to Georgia with the first group of Pietist migrants expelled from Salzburg. Accompanied by his wife Margarethe and his daughter, he became one of the community's leaders. Before he left Austria, he had mined for silver and gold on Gastein's Radhausberg. Like most miners in the Gastein region, he clandestinely practiced Protestantism, owned a few books and read from them in secret conventicles and prayer meetings. But he knew "how to pass as a Catholic" (Melton 54) when he had to. The Jesuits interrogated this "Catholic Evangelical" closely for confessional subterfuge. While he showed himself familiar with Catholic doctrine, his clandestine Protestant activities were revealed in the end, and he and his family were expelled by Archbishop Firmian in 1733. He and his fellow exiles travelled to Augsburg in a caravan of 191 men, women, and children. He and his party accepted the offer to travel to Georgia on September 2 and sailed across the Atlantic to Charleston, SC, and on to Savannah. Geschwandel helped Pastor Boltzius maintain order and mediate conflicts during their 8-week passage. Of the five miners on board, Geschwandel was the only one to survive the first year. Already weakened from their long trip, his wife and daughter died from dysentery during their first year in Ebenezer. Thomas fell on some hard times and took to drinking. He eventually reconciled with Boltzius, and the pastor allowed him to remarry. Having received some good land, he continued to be a community leader and successfully experimented with growing wheat. He died in modest circumstances after a bout with malaria in 1761.

Maria Aloysia Anna von Born (1766-1830)

Maria Aloysia Anna von Born was born in Prague and grew up as a socialite and much-admired beauty in Vienna. She married Count Tommaso von Bassegli from the Republic of Ragusa (Dubrovnik) but returned to Vienna without her husband and eloped with the Swiss-born officer Johann Jakob Ulrich Rivardi to revolutionary France and then to the U.S. in the early 1790s. While Maria entered the salons in Philadelphia, Rivardi took a job with the U.S. Army as a military engineer, fortifying frontier forts destroyed during the American Revolution. She followed him to Fort Clinton (today's West Point) on the New York frontier and married him in 1795 (without annulling her previous marriage with Bassegli). They moved further west to frontier forts in Detroit and then Fort Niagara to lead a life that was far removed from the Vienna palaces she had been used to. The couple had three children. In 1802, Rivardi was honorably dismissed, and Maria now had to rescue the family from ruin. Supported by Presidents Jefferson and Madison, she founded "Madame Rivardi's Seminary for Young Ladies" in Philadelphia, a finishing school for privileged young women. As Jonathan Singerton, her biographer puts it, "Maria created a microcosm of enlightenment and cosmopolitanism." When her second husband died, she was stuck with his debts and ended up in debtors' prison. She returned to Vienna in 1815, after some twenty-five hard years in the U.S. In 1817, she moved to Trieste to be with her son Ulrich, who had relocated his American trading company there, signing her name again as Countess Bassegli. After spending her final years in Italy and France, she died in 1830 (Singerton, *Beginning Her World Anew*).

For more information and multimedia content, visit the book's companion site at www.austriainusa.org

Chapter 2

Growing Contacts in an Age of Mass Migration, 1861-1914

The Habsburg Empire was reformed in 1867 and became the Austrian-Hungarian "Dual" Monarchy. Emperor Francis Joseph had to accommodate the upstart Hungarians. In American History the era between the Civil War and World War I is known as the era of "progressivism" and the age of mass migration (also the "Gilded Age"). Rapid industrialization and urbanization demanded a steady stream of immigrant labor. Between 1900 and 1914, the peoples of the Austro-Hungarian Monarchy constituted the largest immigrant group coming to the United States. After the rocky Austrian-American relationship in the late 1840s and early 1850s due to the pro-Hungarian sentiment in the U.S. and the Mexican adventure by Maximilian during and after the Civil War, relations between the old Empire in Europe and the dynamic new Republic in the New World settled down as both nations pursued their best interests. In the Chicago and St. Louis World Expositions in 1893 and 1904 the Austrian-Hungarian exhibits were spectacular. They highlighted the U.S. presence as a major industrial and political power in the world and signaled American exceptionalism. The Habsburg Monarchy displayed its dramatic industrial growth and modernist arts and craft, including the radically new design of *Secessionism*. The consular network expanded on both sides, and in 1902, finally, the diplomatic representatives were upgraded to the rank of ambassador, reflecting the growing importance of the Austrian-American relationship on the international stage.

Diplomatic relations went through a brief moment of crisis during the first term of President Grover Cleveland (1885-89). Cleveland was a lonely Democrat in a long period of Republican ascendancy from the Civil War to World War I. Republicans respected the Great Power System, as Nicole Phelps contends, while Democrats appointed nonprofessional political hacks to sensitive diplomatic posts.

Mutual perceptions of one another were still negative. Americans regarded the Habsburg government as autocratic, Austrians the U.S. as overly materialistic and uncivilized.

President Grover Cleveland. Austrian-American diplomatic relations went through a brief moment of crisis during President Cleveland's first term, when he nominated Anthony Keiley as U.S. envoy to Vienna without seeking an *agrément* from the Habsburg Court.

When the Cleveland Administration nominated Anthony Keiley as U.S. envoy to Italy without asking for prior agreement from the Italian government (*agrément*), the Italian government refused to receive Keiley because in his earlier career he had given an anti-Italian speech. Cleveland decided to send him instead as envoy to Vienna without seeking an *agrément* from the Habsburg Court. But Vienna also asked Washington not to send Keiley (who was already *en route*) without a prior *agrément* (Phelps, 78). After a long State Department correspondence with Vienna, where Austria-Hungary was called "intolerant, arbitrary, unchivalrous, backward, and uncivilized," the Cleveland Administration reluctantly withdrew Keiley's appointment (Phelps, 81-87). Washington learned from this episode of amateur diplomacy as future appointments were made with prior *agrément*.

With Ladislaus Hengelmüller von Hengervár's (later Baron Hengelmüller) appointment to Washington in 1894, happier times ensued in U.S. – Austrian relations. Hengelmüller represented the Dual Monarchy for almost 20 years until the beginning of the Wilson era in 1913. Hengelmüller and his wife were socially adept, became friends with Theodore Roosevelt, and were darlings of Washington society. Secretary of State Philander Know gave him a warm good-bye by claiming him an "American citizen in every except the technical sense" (Phelps, 89). Hengelmüller tried to mediate growing tensions between the U.S. and Spain in 1898, but had no success. In 1902, he and the American envoy to Vienna were upgraded to "ambassadors."

Mutual perceptions of one another were still negative. Americans regarded the Habsburg government as autocratic, Austrians the U.S. as overly materialistic and uncivilized. Charles Francis Adams Jr., scion of two American presidents, visited the Habsburg Empire in 1873 as the Commonwealth of Massachusetts representative to the Vienna Universal Exposition. He disparaged Vienna as a "city of Jews" and was unimpressed by the Universal Exposition. After visiting the beautiful Tyrolean Alps, he detested the Danube metropole even more. Visiting Hungary, he deemed their peasants and aristocrats "almost barbarous" and added uncharitably: "living almost like the people in the South before the Civil War." Archduke Francis Ferdinand, who visited the U.S. during the Chicago World's Fair in 1893 on his tour around the world, sported similar prejudices. He was unimpressed by the uniform new cities of the American West and was appalled by a "lack of distinguished visitors" at the Chicago World's Fair. However, the electrified exposition at night ("white city") impressed him. But, he found the Americans, lacking any sense of traditional Austrian *"Gemütlichkeit,"* as uncivilized as the Papua New Guineans he had visited on his tour. When Sigmund Freud came on a lecture tour to America in 1909 he was shocked by Americans' materialism, calling America a "gigantic mistake" and "the anti-Paradise." The Archduke and the famous psychiatrist dwelled on traditional European anti-American clichés (Bischof, 27-30).

After the Civil War a growing number of people from the Dual Monarchy migrated to the United States. Initially most of these migrants were Czech families from Bohemia and Vorarlbergers from the Austrian half of the Habsburg Dual Monarchy (Steidl, *Migration Patterns*, 82-86). Before coming to America, Bohemians and Vorarlbergers had long-standing traditions of "border crossing" — the Vorarlbergers to Swabia, the Bohemians to Saxony. While the Bohemians and some Vorarlberg immigrants were very successful, the vast majority of the immigrants from the Monarchy were poor and tried to improve their lives. Towards the end of the 19th century Poles and Jews (from Galicia), Slovaks, Slovenes, Dalmatians, and Hungarians migrated within the Monarchy and/or went to the U.S. for economic reasons.

Emigrants from Austria-Hungary during embarkation on an Austro-Americana vessel in Trieste. The ship depicted is most likely the *S.S. Slavonia*.

Emigrants from Austria-Hungary during embarkation on an Austro-Americana vessel in Trieste.

They found work in the new industrial centers of Pittsburgh, Cleveland, Chicago, and New York. Some went to the western mining centers in Minnesota and Colorado. Between 1890 and 1914, 15 million people left Europe for the U.S., mostly Eastern and Southern Europeans (Steidl *et al.*, 58).

Between 1876 and 1910, some 3.5 million people migrated to the U.S. from the Habsburg Monarchy (1.8 million from the Austrian provinces and 1.7 million from the Hungarian ones); the largest numbers left from the impoverished peripheral provinces of Galicia and Bukovina and from Southern and Eastern Hungary (Steidl *et al.*, 114; Zahra, 25). In the 1900s almost a quarter of all new arrivals to the U.S. were from the Habsburg Monarchy (Agstner, 168). Between 1902 and 1911, 27.9 percent of all migrants to the U.S. came from the Habsburg Monarchy (Steidl, *Migration Patterns*, 79). 7.5 percent of Pittsburgh's half million population came from Austria-Hungary. A surprising 38.5 percent of Austrians (37.9 percent Hungarians) returned home after working in the U.S. for some years (Steidl *et al.*, 69). The age of steamships allowed for such remigration. Many South Slav men came to work in the steel factories and mines in Pennsylvania or on the Iron Range in Minnesota, only to return home after a few years. Some crossed the ocean multiple times (one man 17 times). Between 1908 and 1922 a remarkable 35 percent returned home (Steidl *et al.*, 70, 102). People from the Habsburg Monarchy constituted the largest immigrant cohort in the years before World War I. This massive influx of proletarian "new immigrants" from Eastern (and Southern) Europe produced a nativist backlash in the United States and would lead to immigration restrictions during and after World War I. The Great War stopped this massive migration flow from Central Europe.

In Galicia and Bukovina entire villages were infected from contagious "emigration fever" (Zahra, 25) and traveled on ships from Hamburg and Bremen with HAPAG and *Norddeutscher Lloyd* (and from Trieste with the Austro-Americana shipping line). Tens of thousands of poor Jews left for the New World. Anna Kupinski left Bukovina as an eight-year old for New Jersey: "life was hard in Europe [...] we were poor. We didn't have any luxuries. We hardly had enough food" (Zahra, 34). Surely abject poverty in many backward areas of the empire, lack of land and industrial employment, and escaping military service were principal reasons for being attracted by the lure of America's unlimited riches. By the 1900s the Austrian-Hungarian government tried to staunch the demographic losses incurred by migration to the U.S., making the "migration business" responsible. With the rise of anti-Semitism, Jewish migration agents were blamed for "the exodus of millions"— the "Coolie trade" — in some spectacular trials (Zahra, 43). Women found it particularly difficult to leave since they were assumed to be prostitutes and "white slaves" when they entered the U.S.

A poor migrant's journey to the United States was usually harrowing. If they made it to a migration agent's office, they typically spent a night or two at local hotels or boarding houses at great expense. From there they caught a train to their port of call – Slovaks and Galicians to Hamburg and Bremen, where they might be quarantined before going on board a ship, Croatians and Slovenes mostly to Trieste. Most of these transatlantic travelers were young men and women "in their prime employment age, many of them single and hoping for a profitable job or a suitable marriage partner" (Steidl, *Migration Patterns*, 81). Married men left without families, hoping to make money in the U.S. and returning home to their families (Steidl *et al.*, 69). Starting in 1892, they would have to go through tough health screenings and immigration procedures on New York's Castle Island or Ellis Island (Pollack, 28-35).

A poster advertising Austro-Americana's service from Europe to New York, showing the *Martha Washington*.

Austro-Americana Line

From the first Austrian settlers in Georgia to the big immigration waves in the 19th and early 20th centuries, the dominant method of transportation was the ocean-going ship. The steam engine in particular, as well as subsequent development of ever bigger ocean liners, turned out to be quintessential enablers of European and Austrian emigration in significant numbers.

Many of these big liners in transatlantic service were operated by British, German or Dutch companies, and over the years they carried millions of European emigrants to the United States and Canada, among them many Austrians. However, at the beginning of the 20th century, an Austrian shipping company joined the bee-line from Europe to America and back.

Austro-Americana Line was founded in 1895 by the Austrian hauler Gottfried August Schenker and Scottish shipping merchant William Burell to establish a freight line between Austria and North America, initially with an eye on supplying the Austrian textile and cotton industry. The company was headquartered in the port city of Trieste, Italy, then part of Austria-Hungary. It was also known as *Unione Austriaca di Navigazione*, *Unione Austriaca*, and later as the *Cosulich Line*, but is most commonly referred to as *Austro-Americana*.

Eventually, the company provided both freight and passenger services to many ports in North and South America. The outbreak of World War I marked the looming end for Austro-Americana in its original form: ships were either impounded, shot at by enemy nations or were put into service for the Austrian Navy. After the war, in 1918, only ten ships remained, and since the home port of Trieste came under Italian control, the company was assumed by the Cosulich family, operated as *Cosulich Line* from this point forward and service to the Americas was eventually resumed.

Austro-Americana's *Kaiser Franz Josef I.*

Austro-Americana's *Kaiserin Elisabeth* during construction at Monfalcone shipyard. Due to complications during World War I she was never completed. *Kaiserin Elisabeth* would have been the largest Austrian naval vessel ever built.

The smoking salon for first class passengers aboard Austro-Americana's *Kaiser Franz Josef I*.

An upscale cabin interior on Austro-Americana's *Kaiser Franz Josef I.*

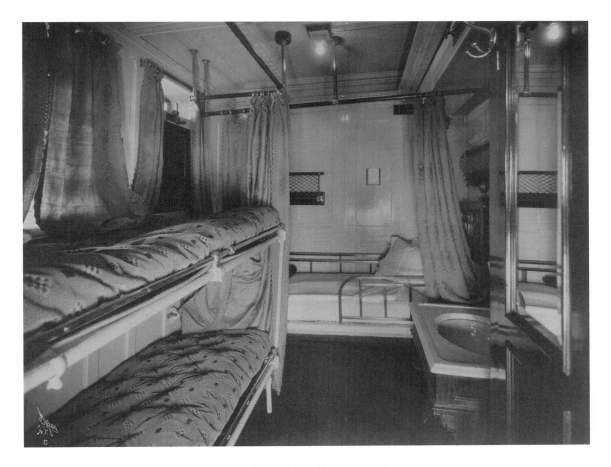

More affordable accommodations aboard the *Kaiser Franz Josef I.*

A dining salon aboard the *Kaiser Franz Josef I.*

A lower class dining facility aboard the *Kaiser Franz Josef I.*

Whale hits liner and kills itself

Raised and Shook *Kaiser Franz Josef*, Over *Titanic* Grave, as if by a Tidal Wave

Headline and article from *The New York Times*, published on July 27, 1913

The Austro-American Liner *Kaiser Franz Josef* came into port yesterday with a large number of passengers, much cargo, and a story of a whale of great proportions, which tried to butt the bottom out of the big liner, and died in the attempt. The Kaiser Franz Josef was shaken to such an extent that the skipper, all of his junior officers, half of the crew, and scores of the passengers rushed on deck in apprehension. Not until the dead body of the giant mammal was seen floating away to windward did the skipper and his men know what had been under them.

The account of the whale is vouched for by no less an authority than Gustav Millimoth, the First Officer of the Kaiser Franz Josef, who at the time of the commotion happened to be entering on the log the fact that the big liner was at the moment passing over the grave of the *Titanic*. While he was still making his entry, the liner suddenly lurched upward, as if lifted by a tidal wave. The ship shook from the stern, and Capt. Gerolomich, who was in his cabin, jumped to the bridge.

The passengers deserted smoker room lounges and the state room and crowded the decks. In about five minutes the cause of all the trouble floated from under the ship. It was a whale at least seventy feet long, and a great gash in the middle of his back showed what the collision with the steamship had done to it. Those of the passengers who had cameras snapshotted the dead monster, and these photographs were shown yesterday. They showed a giant whale floating in the water, and a close look made it possible to see the great wound that ended his life.

The Kaiser Franz Josef had among her passengers the Baron Bela von Hazan, a son of the Hungarian Minister of War. Baron von Hazan is here on a short vacation, the principal object of which is a chance to view Niagara Falls. He saw the whale.

Ellis Island, ca. 1900. The U.S. government barred immigrants who were sick, suspicious, had criminal records, or were likely to become "public charges."

At the entrance of the New World, ca. 1900.
The photograph shows a male immigrant standing
in front of the door with all his possessions.

Ellis Island, ca. 1915. An immigrant girl and boy with belongings.

Between 1876 and 1910, some 3.5 million people migrated to the U.S. from the Habsburg Monarchy (1.8 million from the Austrian provinces and 1.7 million from the Hungarian ones).

Pittsburgh, Pennsylvania, July 2, 1915. Panoramic view of downtown, with rail yards, river, and coal barges. Many poor immigrants from the Habsburg Monarchy searched for opportunities in the industrial centers on the East Coast and the Midwest. Between 1902 and 1911, some 7.5 percent of Pittsburgh's population came from Austria-Hungary.

Mesabi Range, Minnesota, 1905. Two men standing in front of a shaft house and a railroad car filled with iron ore.

Mesabi Range, Minnesota, 1903. Miners at work on the Mesabi range in northeast Minnesota.

Cleveland, Ohio, between 1900 and 1910.
The photo shows Cleveland Harbor. Just like Pittsburgh, Cleveland attracted many immigrants from Austria-Hungary in search of work. Hard labor in industry and coal were not the exception.

The U.S. Government barred migrants who were sick, suspicious, had criminal records, or were "likely to become public charges." Single women, unless they planned to work as domestic servants, were assumed "to become public charges" (Zahra, 40). 1.2 to 2 percent of immigrants were rejected on Ellis Island (Steidl, *Border Control*). Some were quarantined after medical examinations — "high fences" protecting America from such tainted migrants (Zahra, 41). Only once they made it past Ellis Island, did they travel to the places of their choice, where they had family or expected to get work. Where did they settle? That depended on economic opportunities. Cheap train fares were to be had from New York City into all directions (Steidl, *Border Control*). The Czechs of the first wave joined Germans and Scandinavians to settle on the agricultural frontier in the Midwest and Texas. The Poles, Slovaks, Jews and Hungarians who came at the turn of the century went to the new industrial centers on the East Coast (Pennsylvania) or the Midwest (Cleveland, Chicago).

Thousands of these poor migrants were injured or died in work accidents in coal mines and in steel plants. One anti-emigration activist in Austria contended that 33,000 Austro-Hungarian citizens were killed on the job in American industrial accidents each year, and that another 10,000 were murdered annually (Zahra, 52), surely a gross exaggeration. Austrian diplomatic representatives had to deal regularly with migrants from the Monarchy that had come to harm in work accidents. While immigration agents and boosters of migration talked up the endless opportunities in the U.S., consulates knew better from the many serious work accidents reported year after year. People were killed and maimed and were often not compensated and left without any means. If they returned to Austria-Hungary, they became "public charges" (Phelps, 103-70).

In 1897, 18 striking workers, Polish and Hungarian subjects of the Habsburg Monarchy who had not obtained U.S. citizenship yet, were protesting poor working conditions, bad wages, and the recent imposition of an Alien Tax on immigrant workers in the Pennsylvania coal mines. They were killed by a local sheriff's posse in Lattimer, PA. Put on trial and acquitted of all charges, the sheriff declared that "this was a victory for America." After consular officials studied the incident and wrote a report to the U.S. State Department, the Austrian-Hungarian government demanded that the U.S. pay an indemnity for the loss of life. After the acquittal of the local sheriff, the U.S. government refused to pay an indemnity to the Austro-Hungarian government (McDowell, *Price of Sovereignty*).

The Chicago (1893) and St. Louis (1904) World Expositions were spectacular affairs displaying the United States' new presence in the world as a premier industrial power and American exceptionalism. The 1893 Chicago World's Fair was called "the Columbian Exposition," celebrating the 400th anniversary of Christopher Columbus's arrival in the New World. Chicago also wanted to show to the world that it literally had risen from the ashes after the great fire of 1871. The spectacular exhibit grounds and its illumination at night gave Chicago the reputation of being "the white city." Twelve major buildings and dozens of smaller ones for international and American states exhibits went up for the Columbian Exposition in barely two years. Built by thousands of laborers under harsh conditions, some of them surely hailed from the Habsburg Monarchy. The Chicago World's Fair was designed to outdo the glamorous 1889 Paris *Exposition Universelle* (Larson). Twenty-seven million people visited the Chicago Columbian Exposition on grounds covering 690 acres (2.8 km²) during its six-month run (May to October). The 200 buildings constructed were mostly temporary structures. Forty-six nations displayed the best of their home-made products, Austria was one of them.

The Chicago (1893) and St.Louis (1904) World Expositions were spectacular affairs displaying the United States' new presence in the world as a premier industrial power and American exceptionalism.

Chicago World's Fair 1893. View of the Art Palace.

Chicago World's Fair 1893. Manufacture Building, main portal of the Austrian section.

Chicago World's Fair 1893. The Austrian Commission Building, Edgerton Avenue.

Chicago World's Fair 1893. Manufacture Building. General view of the Austrian section, as seen from the gallery.

Chicago World's Fair 1893. Manufacture Building. The presentation of jeweler and silversmith Georg A. Scheid is at center; porcelain by Ernst Wahliss is shown in the background (left and right).

Chicago World's Fair 1893. View of the lagoons, looking north.

Chicago World's Fair 1893. Manufacture Building, presentation of the Austrian *A. Förster* company.

The spectacular exhibit grounds and its illumination at night gave Chicago the reputation of being "the white city."

In Chicago only the Austrian half of the Dual Monarchy was represented. Hungary stayed away, instead concentrating on its Millennial Exposition to be held in Budapest in 1896. The Chicago organizers allotted Austria almost 90,000 square feet of space, of which more than half was used in the gigantic Manufactures and Liberal Arts Building. The Austrian government devoted 275,000 florins to pay for sending and staging the exhibits. Elaborate committees were established in Vienna and Chicago under the protection of Archduke Carl Ludwig, the emperor's younger brother, to select hundreds of exhibitors from all over the Austrian half of the Dual Monarchy in all fields of Austrian economic activity (for the lists see *Amtlicher Special-Katalog*). The Austrian exhibits were characterized by "a queer mixture of the medieval and the modern" (*Austria on Display*, 123). The Austrian exhibits of "china, gold and silver medallion, bronze and enameled tiles" impressed most visitors. Moreover, "some of the handsomest curtains" were to be found in the Austrian exhibits, next to outstanding porcelain, wood carvings, as well as faience and enamel ware (*Austria on Display*, 122-23). People were particularly taken in by the glass production of Bohemia. Two outstanding Bohemian vases were featured with faithful pictures of significant American historical events: the Declaration of Independence, the discovery of electricity and steam power, and the abolition of slavery, featuring Lincoln and his cabinet (*Austria on Display*, 123-25). Next to industrial and artistic productions, agriculture was represented, too with displays of cultivation of bees, hops, mineral water, liqueurs, and wine. On August 18 — Emperor Francis Joseph's birthday — an elaborate parade was staged on the festival grounds, featuring floats with various representatives of the Austrian and Hungarian community in Chicago (*Austria on Display*, 126-27).

St. Louis has lost out to Chicago for the 1893 world's fair but managed to get the 1904 fair. Named the "Louisiana Purchase Exposition" commemorating the 100th anniversary of Jefferson's Louisiana Purchase, the fair lasted from April to November 1904 and had almost 20 million visitors. Fifty foreign nations and 43 of the then 45 states exhibited in some 1,500 buildings on 1,200 acres (almost five km^2). Austria decided very late to participate in the 1904 exposition and opened its pavilion a month late, in June 1904. Austria wanted to display its "schools of artistic industry" and impressed with its great interior designs of the Secession movement. Josef Hoffmann's design of a room devoted to the paintings of Gustav Klimt as a *Gesamtkunstwerk* was turned down by the Ministry of Culture (McClain, 46-49). Aurora McClain has pieced together the 13 rooms of the Austrian exhibit (McClain, App. B, 101). Ludwig Baumann, Archduke Franz Ferdinand's favorite architect, designed the Austrian pavilion, with references both to the historical and the Secessionist style. The first two rooms designed by Otto Wagner students were strikingly modern (most of these objects were bought during the Exposition). Josef Hoffmann designed the room of the Vienna Arts and Crafts School and displayed one of the earliest examples of Secessionism in the United States. Students displayed objects in this room, raising the level of decorative arts to new levels. The Prague School of Arts and Crafts, designed by Jan Kotěra, yet another Wagner student, displayed the *Jugendstil* in full flower. It also demonstrated how much Prague arts and crafts had a close relationship with industry (McClain, 59). Rooms dedicated to Bohemian and Polish artists also displayed Secessionist elements.

St. Louis World's Fair, 1904.
View of the Austrian Pavilion.

St. Louis World's Fair, 1904. View of the Austrian Pavilion.

St. Louis World's Fair, 1904. President Theodore Roosevelt and David R. Francis leaving the Austrian Building on Roosevelt Day, November 26, 1904.

Ludwig Baumann (1853 – 1936). Archduke Franz Ferdinand's favorite architect designed the Austrian Pavilion in St. Louis with references to both the historical and the Secessionist style.

McClain also has analyzed the reception of the Austrian Pavilion. Reviewers praised the innovative and creative designs of the exhibit and the Austrian Arts and Crafts School but some found these new designs too radical. Other critics were enthusiastic and found Austrian *Art Nouveau* "charming," commenting "the Austrians have most certainly broken away from old traditions, and have produced something very original and refined." The relationship between artists and industry and their "push to make design more accessible for everyone" impressed democratic Americans (McClain, 65-66). The rave American reviews about the Austrian Pavilion were more impressed with interior design than the exterior of the building, Austria's commercially successful design products showed that "art is not only an ornament but an excellent investment" (McClain, 67). Americans might take note of these dramatically modern and handsome Austrian designs for their own homes rather than lavish their money on "the wearisome copies of Italian Renaissance, Louis XV, and Louis XVI" (McClain, 69). Seeing these striking Austrian design exhibits it dawned on Americans that they were lagging far behind in industrial arts. Some local St. Louis architects began incorporating some of the Secessionist elements like simplified facades with minimal ornamentation in houses they built in their city (McClain, 70- 75). The Austrian exhibits in St. Louis thus left lasting legacies in the U.S.

Reviewers praised the innovative and creative designs of the exhibit and the Austrian Arts and Crafts School but some found these new designs too radical. Other critics were enthusiastic and found Austrian *Art Nouveau* "charming," commenting "the Austrians have most certainly broken away from old traditions, and have produced something very original and refined."

Franz Martin Drexel

Franz Martin Drexel, a trained painter from Dornbirn, Vorarlberg, first had some success as a portraitist in Philadelphia. In 1837 he began to deal in foreign currencies in Louisville and started the banking house of F.M. Drexel in Philadelphia in the 1840s, adding an office in San Francisco to make a fortune in the gold rush. With his two sons, Franz Martin developed his bank into one of the most successful banking houses in the U.S., also cooperating with America's premier financier J.P. Morgan. In 1891 the Drexels endowed an institute that eventually became Drexel University in Philadelphia. Drexel's granddaughter Katharine Drexel became a nun and financed some 60 schools in African-American ghettoes and Native-American reservations from her inheritance. In 1924 she founded Xavier University in New Orleans, the first black college in the U.S. In 2000, the Vatican canonized Saint Katherine.

Johann Michael Kohler

Johann Michael Kohler migrated with his family from Schnepfau, Vorarlberg, to Minnesota where he farmed in 1864. His son Michael, one of eight children, moved to Chicago, Illinois, married well and moved to Sheboygan, Wisconsin. First working in the iron industry, he began producing enamel ware, such as pots, bath tubs, and water closets. By 1900 Kohler Company, in the company town of Kohler Village, employed some 4,000 workers producing enameled toilets and bath tubs for the growing American middle class. The Kohler company became also known for authoritarian anti-union labor practices. Kohler's son Herbert was elected governor of Wisconsin in the 1920s and his son Herbert, Jr. in the 1960s. The Kohler Company is still in family hands today and employs some 15,000 people.

Mendel Beck

Mendel Beck was 25 years old and left his Eastern Galician hometown Lisko/Linsk in May 1888. Fourteen percent of the population of Eastern Galicia was Jewish and desperately poor, lacking jobs, food and adequate clothing. He made his living as a shoemaker who travelled around his hometown to repair shoes. With industrially produced cheap shoes and boots being imported to Galicia from Vienna and Bohemia, he lost business. Becoming an *"Amerikageher"* – looking for a better life was the last option left for this young man. He saved up money to leave for New York with a friend and three other young men. He took the train to Cracow and Oświęcin/Auschwitz, where they bought tickets for the ship passage from Hamburg to New York. Overcharged by the Jewish agents, they made it to Hamburg and onto a HAPAG ship to New York. After two weeks on board an over-crowded ship and sea sick, they made it to New York, where upon arrival they were frisked and interrogated at the Castle Garden immigration station and pushed through like cattle. They finally made it on shore to New York, where their traces were lost (Pollack, 22-31, 66-88).

For
info
and
con
visit
com
site
aust

more
mation
multimedia
ent,
the book's
panion
at www.
riainusa.org

Chapter 3

The Age of the World Wars, 1914-1945

The age of the two World Wars was the most contentious time in Austrian-American bilateral relations. It happened to be the time when Austria-Hungary on the side of Wilhelmine Germany, as well as Austria as part of Hitler's Third Reich, directly fought against the United States. Yet Austrians kept coming to the U.S. to look for better fortunes in their lives. There was a sizable group of people from the Burgenland who came in the early 1920s before the issuing of the "quota laws" of 1921/1924. In spite of these laws, thousands of Jews managed to migrate to the U.S. after the Nazi takeover of Austria in 1938 (*Anschluss*). Thousands of these people in exile volunteered for the U.S. armed forces and the intelligence services during World War II to make their personal contribution to the liberation of their homeland from the Nazi occupation.

World War I quickly stopped the era of mass migration from the Habsburg lands to the U.S. President Woodrow Wilson committed the U.S. to a policy of neutrality in the war raging throughout the European continent, when it broke out in July 1914. Due to the Dual Alliance entered into in 1879, Austria-Hungary fought on the side of Germany and thus was pulled more deeply into the war vis-à-vis the U.S. when German submarines started to sink enemy ships to counter the British blockade of the continent. When the *Lusitania* was sunk in May 1915 and more than a thousand people perished (among them more than one hundred Americans), Wilson threatened to break relations with Germany. In November 1915 the German U-38, sailing under the "Austrian" flag, sunk the Italian passenger ship *SS Ancona* in the Mediterranean killing 200 people (among them nine Americans). Austria received a stern protest from the U.S. and the demand for restitution, but the U.S. never threatened to break relations with the Habsburg Monarchy. What the Americans did not know was that a German U-boat had sunk the *Ancona*. Since Germany was not at war with Italy, the Austrians practiced "preventive diplomacy" and allowed the world to believe it was an Austrian submarine (Bednar, 265-67).

German submarine U-38 was sailing under Austrian flag in 1915 when it torpedoed and sunk the Italian passenger liner *SS Ancona*, killing 200 people, among them nine Americans.

Undated photograph of U-38 captioned "In safe water. Refreshing bath of air in the morning after exhausting night-cruise."

At this time, Austria-Hungary no longer had an ambassador in Washington. With the outbreak of the war, the U.S. government spied on the Austrian and German diplomatic representatives, tapped their telephone lines and capped their transatlantic cables. Ambassador Konstantin Dumba, unlike his likable predecessor Henglmüller, was considered "arrogant and condescending." He had been declared *persona non grata* in September 1915, after he had been accused of spying and coming up with a scheme to sabotage the American munitions industry. President Wilson never received his successor Count Tarnowski thus preventing him from doing his job. When the U.S. declared war on the Dual Monarchy in December 1917 (half a year after going to war with Germany over its resumption of unrestricted submarine warfare), the United States and Austria-Hungary no longer had official channels of communications with one another. The American ambassador Frederick Penfield had been recalled in the fall of 1915 too. Wilson declared war on the Dual Monarchy since he felt they were lackeys of the Germans (Phelps, 222-31).

American military forces only clashed with the armies of Austria-Hungary late in the war. Austria-Hungary fought most of their engagements with the Russians in the East, the Serbs in the Balkans, and the Italians high in the Alps. Only in July 1918 did Austria-Hungary send four infantry divisions to the Western front, where 8,300 soldiers from the Monarchy were killed, maimed, or became prisoners of war. An American regiment participated in the final Italian offensive on the Southern front in late October 1918, resulting in the armistice a few days later. American volunteer ambulance drivers such as the writer Ernest Hemingway encountered "Austrian" troops. He was wounded and wrote about his experiences in his novel *A Farewell to Arms* (Bednar, 267-69).

American military forces only clashed with the armies of Austria-Hungary late in the war. Austria-Hungary fought most of their engagements with the Russians in the East, the Serbs in the Balkans, and the Italians high in the Alps.

Ladislaus Henglmüller
Ladislaus Henglmüller von Hengervar served as Ambassador of Austria-Hungary to the United States from October 1894 until January 1913. His tenure included the Presidential administrations of William McKinley, Theodore Roosevelt, and William Taft.

Shown here in ca. 1900 at the Austrian-Hungarian Embassy in Washington, DC, Henglmüller became a well-liked member of Washington society and a personal friend of President Theodore Roosevelt.

Konstantin Dumba, Ladislaus Henglmüller's successor as Ambassador of Austria-Hungary to the United States, was declared *persona non grata* by President Wilson in September 1915 amidst accusations of espionage and sabotage.

Given this lack of military engagements, the Austrian Foreign Minister Ottokar Czernin characterized the U.S. – Austrian interactions during the war a "paper war."

President Wilson's principal actions vis-à-vis Austria-Hungary came with his role in breaking up the Habsburg Monarchy. On January 8, 1918, he presented his 14-Points as his principal contribution to the American postwar peace program. Point No. 10 proclaimed: "The people of Austria-Hungary, whose place among the nations we wish to see safeguarded and assured, should be accorded the freest opportunity to autonomous development." Wishing to "safeguard" Austria-Hungary, and granting autonomy to its peoples was a contradictory statement. Kurt Bednar denounces President Wilson's "self-determination" as his "poison pill." Wilson's academic experts in his advisory body "the Inquiry" – even though none of them was an expert on the Habsburg Monarchy - began advocating for the formation of the new nation states Czechoslovakia, Yugo-Slavia, and Poland in Central Europe (Bednar, 285-341).

Based on racialist thinking in the American government and Wilson's principle of "self-determination," the Wilson Administration advocated for homogeneous national communities. It willy-nilly accepted the break-up of the autocratic Habsburg Monarchy with its support of these new democratic nation states when they proclaimed their independence from the Habsburg Monarchy in October 1918. Wilson's decisions were reinforced by strong ethnic Bohemian, Slovak, Polish, and South Slav lobbies in the U.S. Given these strong ethnic lobbies in the U.S. and the lack of Austrian diplomatic representation throughout 1917/18, the Wilson Administration was no longer willing to mediate in the Habsburg lands, when Emperor Charles suggested a "federalist" solution late in the war (Phelps, 231-57).

Based on racialist thinking in the American government and Wilson's principle of "self-determination," the Wilson Administration advocated for homogeneous national communities. It willy-nilly accepted the break-up of the autocratic Habsburg Monarchy with its support of these new democratic nation states when they proclaimed their independence from the Habsburg Monarchy in October.

Embassy of Austria-Hungary in Washington, DC In late 1895, Austria-Hungary purchased a large mansion to house both the legation and the residence of the Ambassador. It was located at 1305 Connecticut Avenue, just south of Dupont Circle, and had been built by David Levy Yulee, the first Jewish Senator in the U.S. Congress.

Picture taken between 1909 and 1920.

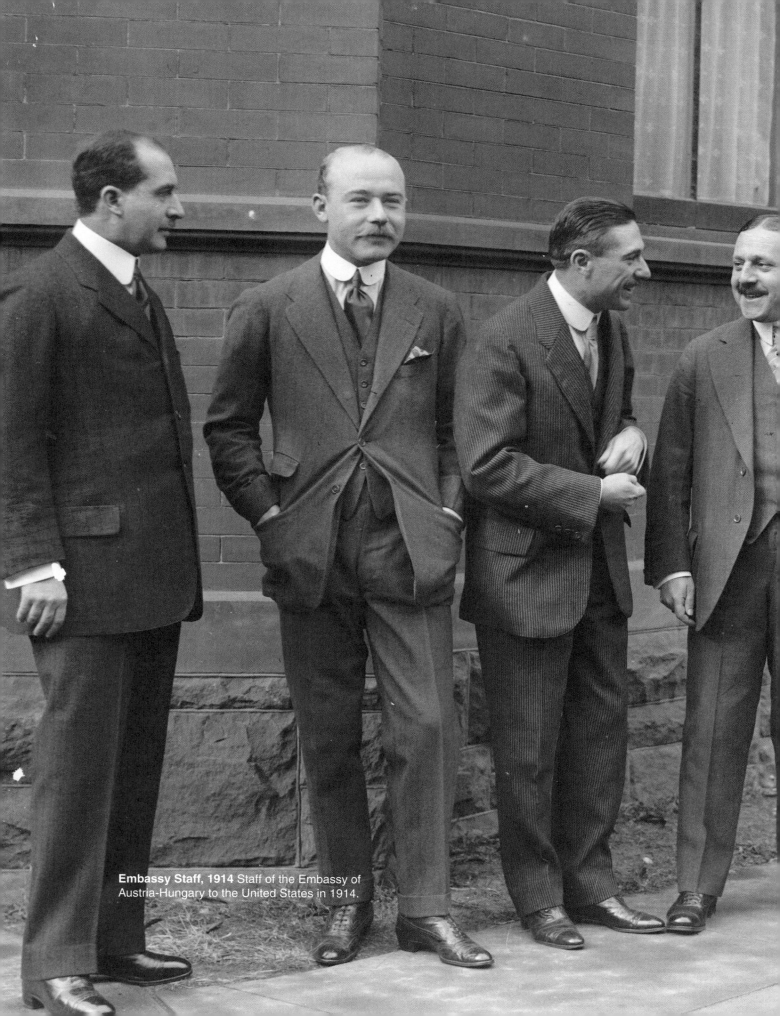

Embassy Staff, 1914 Staff of the Embassy of Austria-Hungary to the United States in 1914.

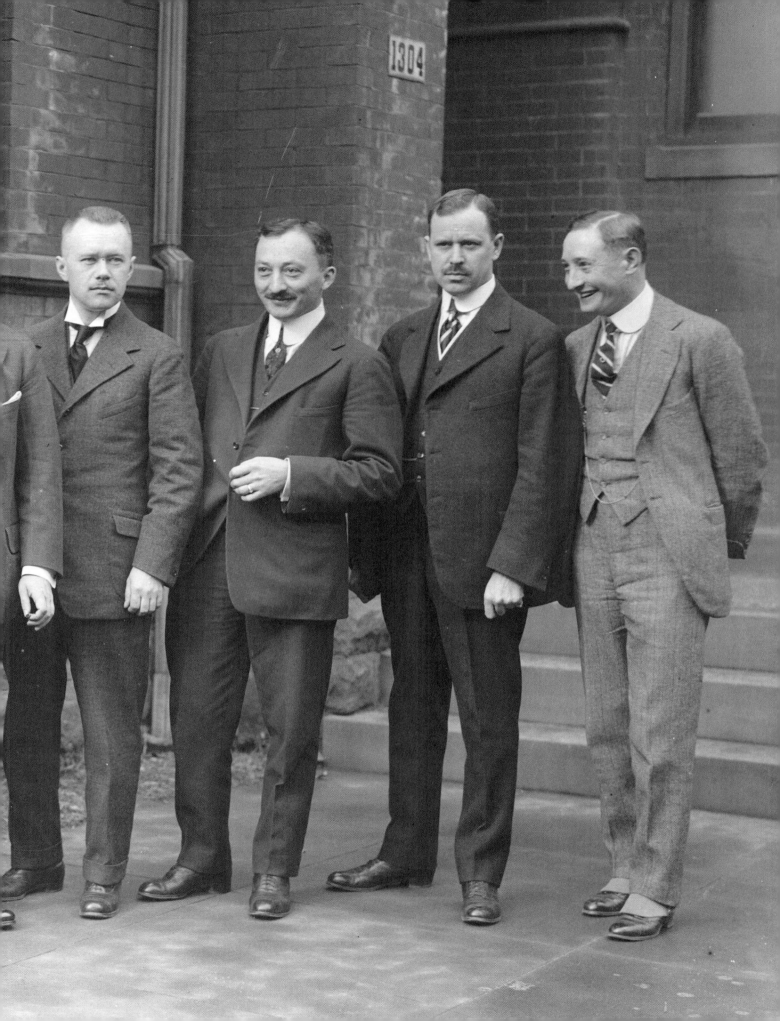

Embassy Interior, ca. 1893 Interior view of a salon at the Austrian Embassy, ca. 1893.
According to the Congressional Directory, the location of the residence and legation was listed at
1410 Connecticut Avenue from 1887 until 1895.

Embassy Interior, ca. 1893 View of a salon inside the Austrian Embassy in Washington, DC, ca. 1893.

President Wilson came to Europe to preside over the Paris Peace Conference. He was cheered wildly on his visits to Paris, Rome, and London, but did not visit Vienna or Berlin, the capitals of the defeated powers. The "Inquiry" experts (usually relying on anti-Habsburg British expertise) served on the American Commission to Negotiate Peace in Paris and completed the dissolution of the Habsburg Monarchy with the drawing of new borders in Central Europe, not always responding to the argument of clear ethnic-linguistic borders as was the case with the German-speaking South Tyrol given to Italy (Phelps, 248-57). In the spring of 1919 an American Commission headed by the Harvard historian Archibald Cary Coolidge visited Vienna, supporting plebiscites in the drawing of the Austrian borders. Even though the Americans would have accepted the *Anschluss* (annexation) of the new German rump-state of Austria to Germany, the French and Austria's neighbors were dead-set against it (Bednar, 380-433). So the prohibition of *Anschluss* was written into the peace treaty with Austria signed in the Paris suburb on St. Germain. This prohibition, more than anything else, soured American relations with post-World War I Austria and Germany, making both of them "revisionist" powers.

On October 21, 1918, before the end of the war, the ethnic German deputies to the Austrian parliament *(Reichsrat)* elected in 1911 met and proclaimed themselves to be a "Provisional National Assembly for German-Austria." Emperor Karl abdicated on November 11, when the armistice was signed, and tolerated the proclamation of the new German-Austrian Republic on November 12, 1918. The Treaty of St. Germain with Austria, however, prohibited Anschluss with Germany. The U.S. only recognized the new Republic in the summer of 1921, when Washington resumed diplomatic relations with the new Republic of Austria (after a four-year hiatus).

The Americans and Woodrow Wilson's principle of "self-determination" served as the principal architects of the break-up of the Habsburg Monarchy. Yet under Herbert Hoover's America Relief Administration the hungry Austrian population and the children of Vienna were saved from starvation with food shipments from the American Relief Administration from 1919 to 1923 ("Hoover Aid"). Food aid was used to immunize Austrians against the "Communist virus" and contain communism from spilling over from Hungary (Bela Kun Administration) to Central Europe.

Woodrow Wilson

Frederic Penfield Frederic Courtland Penfield served as the United States Minister to Austria from July 1913 until April 1917.

Ernst Kunwald Dr. Ernst Kunwald, an immigrant from Vienna, Austria, was the conductor of the Cincinnati Symphony Orchestra from 1912 until 1917.

He is seen here entering the Federal Building in Cincinnati, Ohio as a prisoner of war on December 8, 1917. Kunwald is escorted by two U.S. Deputy Marshalls. He was released the following day and re-arrested on January 12, 1918, interned under the Alien Enemies Act in Fort Oglethorpe in Georgia, and subsequently deported.

"The question of the independence of Austria has become the primary factor in the maintenance of peace in Europe."

- George Messersmith, United States Minister to Austria (1934-1937)

George Messersmith George Messersmith served as the United States Minister in Vienna from 1934 – 1937 and witnessed the rise of the Nazis first-hand. He warned President Roosevelt about Nazi pressure on Austria as early as 1934.

Messersmith is depicted here as Assistant Secretary of State, delivering an address of welcome to industrialists from around the world in Washington, DC on September 19, 1938.

The Americans and Woodrow Wilson's principle of "self-determination" served as the principal architects of the break-up of the Habsburg Monarchy. Yet under Herbert Hoover's America Relief Administration the hungry Austrian population and the children of Vienna were saved from starvation with food shipments from the American Relief Administration from 1919 to 1923 ("Hoover Aid"). Food aid was used to immunize Austrians against the "Communist virus" and contain communism from spilling over from Hungary (Bela Kun Administration) to Central Europe (Adlgasser).

In spite of growing xenophobia and nativism during World War I vis-à-vis migrants, the United States remained the principal attraction for would-be immigrants. Some 24,000 people from the Burgenland – the territory of Western Hungary that became Austrian in 1920 – migrated to the U.S., mainly for economic reasons. Before World War I some 33,000 *Burgenländers* (then Hungarians) came to the U.S. as part of the mass migration from the Habsburg Monarchy to the U.S. Most of them settled in the industrial centers of the Midwest, especially in Chicago, where today 30,000 *Burgenländers* and their descendants live (Strobl). In 1924 Congress passed the Johnson-Reed Act and introduced a quota system in U.S. immigration law. The law was designed to staunch the flow of "new immigrants" from Southern and Eastern Europe who were perceived to be "non-whites" and non-assimilable. Austria, being considered an "Eastern" European country, received a small quota. This slowed down the flow of immigrants from Burgenland considerably. While in 1922 and 1923 10,255 people from the Burgenland came to the United States, from 1924 to 1934 only 3,408 persons were admitted.

The principal Austrian political parties supported *Anschluss* in the 1920s. When Engelbert Dollfuss got rid of Parliament in 1933 and established an authoritarian government, he advocated for a non-German Austrian identity (and thus promoted an anti-*Anschluss* stance). After his assassination by the Austrian Nazis in the summer of 1934, his successor Kurt Schuschnigg continued this agenda. After Hitler's seizure of power in Germany in 1933, Berlin's pressure on the Schusschnigg government increased enormously. In the "July Agreement" of 1936 and Hitler's meeting with Schuschnigg in Berchtesgaden in February 1938, Nazi pressure on Austria grew even further. On March 12, 1938 the Wehrmacht invaded Austria and annexed the country *(Anschluss)*. Now the "Ostmark" was incorporated into the Third Reich.

George Messersmith, the American Minister in Vienna (1934-37), who had witnessed the rise of the Nazis as the American consul in Berlin (1930-33), warned Washington about Nazi pressure on Austria. As early as 1934, this American Cassandra in Central Europe warned the Roosevelt Administration: "The question of the independence of Austria has become the primary factor in the maintenance of the peace in Europe" (Bischof, *Austria's Loss – America's Gain*, 61). Messersmith also warned about growing anti-Semitism in Vienna. However, the Roosevelt Administration was mired in the economic throes of the great depression and had to cope with growing isolationism as expressed through the Congressional neutrality legislation. Congress restricted the White House's room to maneuver vis-à-vis the growing threats of war in Europe and Asia (Berteau). Roosevelt's State Department therefore continued American appeasement of the Third Reich during the Austrian crisis and recognized the *Anschluss* quickly de facto (never *de jure*) (Keyserlingk, 23-26).

Many Jews committed suicide, or left the country to save their lives (Flügge, 295-346). Joseph Goebbels happily wrote in his diary on March 13 1938: "most of the Jews have fled. Whereto? As eternal Jews into Nothingness" [*Als ewige Juden ins Nichts*] (Flügge, 295). The American Minister in Vienna John Wiley – the Embassy was downgraded to a consulate – worked overtime to process the papers of Jews who stood in long lines in front of the U.S. consulate in Vienna to immigrate to the U.S. Going back to the immigration reforms of 1924, the Austrian quota was only 1,435 *per annum* and was now rolled into the larger German quota. Eventually some 30,000 of the 205,000 Austrian Jews managed to migrate to the United States. Among them were many prominent academics who found jobs in American universities as well as the youngsters Frederic Morton, who would become a famous non-fiction writer, and Raul Hilberg, the future godfather of Holocaust historiography (Bischof, *Finis Austriae*, in: Bischof, Beziehunggeschichten, 67-74). Among them was also Heinz Grünwald who managed to obtain a visa with his parents for the U.S. against all odds. What he left behind ruefully were the places where he grew up: "the nursery, the playgrounds, the friends, the secret dreams and rituals of childhood, childhood itself" (Grunwald, 29). He reinvented himself as Henry Grunwald on the Upper Westside of New York City (see portrait in Ch. 6).

As many as 6,000 to 7,000 Austrians in exile in the United States joined the U.S. military and/or the Office of Strategic Services (OSS), the U.S. civilian intelligence service during World War II (the predecessor to the postwar CIA) (Traussnig, 16). These Austrians became Americans—"leaning on" the U.S. to participate in the defeat of Adolf Hitler's Third Reich. Among them were the soldiers who signed up for the aborted "Austrian Battalion". It was Otto von Habsburg's idea: The War Department established the Austrian Battalion in November 1942, and President Roosevelt disbanded it in May 1943 due to a lack of recruits (Traussnig, 26-90).

Emboldened by the *Anschluss*, homegrown Austrian Nazis began persecuting their Jewish neighbors. They humiliated the Jews by forcing them to clean the streets of Vienna with toothbrushes, they stole their property ("aryanizations") – apartments, cars, works of art, businesses.

Edgar L.G. Prochnik

Edgar Prochnik served as Austrian Minister to the United States from 1921 until Austria's Anschluss to Hitlerite Germany. "A man without a country" after 40 years in diplomatic service, Prochnik terminated his service at the (now) German Embassy and instead lectured at Georgetown University's School of Foreign Service.

He is pictured here on September 20, 1938 with a plaque presented to him by Georgetown University earlier.

As many as 6,000 – 7,000 expatriate Austrians joined the U.S. military and/or the Office of Strategic Services (OSS) during World War II.

The U.S. Army recruited thousands of Central European exiles to be trained at the "Military Intelligence Training Center" in Camp Ritchie, Maryland. Known as the "Ritchie Boys," most of them were involved in POW interrogations in the European theater of operations.

Many Austrians in exile were drafted into the 10th Mountain Division, an elite unit in the U.S. Army that saw some heavy fighting in Northern Italy toward the end of the war. Among them was Friedl Pfeiffer, who had been a member of the Austrian National Ski Racing Team. A ski instructor from St. Anton, who first came to Sun Valley, Idaho, Pfeiffer ended up in the 10th and was wounded badly in Italy in April 1945. After the war he became a founder of the Aspen, Colorado, winter resort (Traussnig, 151-206).

The U.S. Army recruited thousands of Central European exiles to be trained at the "Military Intelligence Training Center" in Camp Ritchie, Maryland. Known as the "Ritchie Boys," most of them were involved in POW interrogations in the European theater of operations. The approximately 300 Austrians in exile who served in the American intelligence unit "Office of Strategic Services" (OSS) may be the most distinguished group. Many worked in the propaganda division of the OSS "Morale Operations Branch" and utilized their many talents in producing effective propaganda against the Third Reich, among them the young Viennese Socialist and anti-fascist Rudolf Anzböck. The OSS's Labor Section recruited the Social Democrat. He served as a research analyst in London, assessing everyday life in Nazi Germany (Traussnig, 93-150).

From their bases in England and North Africa (later Southern Italy), the American 8th and 15th Army Air Forces had pounded Nazi occupied Austria from the air since the fall off 1943. Most major Austrian cities had been ruined and many factories destroyed. In the winter/spring of 1945 civilian populations were increasingly targeted. The population on the ground retaliated by "lynching" some 100 American airmen that had bailed out of their planes being shot down, as a recent study by Georg Hoffman has shown.

Based on American intelligence picked up from sources inside the Third Reich, General Dwight D. Eisenhower, the Supreme Commander of Allied Forces, was afraid that Hitler would make his last stance in an Austrian-Bavarian "Alpine Fortress" (*Alpenfestung*) and prolong the fighting for another year. Eisenhower therefore turned his armies conquering Germany southward to preempt such a "last stand" by Nazi fanatics.

Karl Lazarsfeld (1901-1976)

Karl Lazarsfeld was the founder of Columbia University's Bureau of Applied Social Research, exerting a major influence over the techniques and the organization of social research. Born to well-situated Jewish parents in Vienna and active in the Socialist Youth Movement, he attended the University of Vienna, where he received a doctorate in mathematics. He came to sociology through his expertise in mathematics and statistical methods, participating in several early quantitative studies. He and his first wife Marie Jahoda and Hans Zeisel wrote the sociological classic on the social impact of unemployment on a small community -- *Die Arbeitslosen von Marienthal* (1932; English ed. 1971). The Rockefeller Foundation gave him a two-year traveling fellowship to the United States. From 1933-1935, Lazarsfeld worked with the Federal Emergency Relief Administration, visiting the few universities that had programs related to empirical social science research across the U.S. He met the eminent sociologist Robert S. Lynd, who had written the *Middletown* study and would come to play a central role in helping Lazarsfeld gain citizenship in the United States. Lazarsfeld briefly returned to Vienna in 1935. Given the rise of Austro-fascism, he returned to the U.S. and became director of the Newark Center, perfecting his empirical research methodology. He then moved to the Princeton Office of Radio Research, which moved to Columbia University. By 1940 it grew into the acclaimed Bureau for Social Research. At Columbia, Lazarsfeld directed his research towards voting behavior, public opinion, and market research. He trained dozens of graduate students and is considered a founding figure of quantitative modern American sociology (Fleck).

Josef Buttinger (1906-1992)

Josef Buttinger rose as a politician in the Austrian labor movement and became a refugee helper during and after World War II. Born into a working-class family, he left school at age 13 to help support his family. Self-taught, he became a leader in the Socialist Youth Movement and, by the age of 24, had become a secretary of the Social Democratic Party. Imprisoned for several months after the February uprising in 1934, he became chairman of the anti-Fascist Socialist underground. He became friends with the wealthy American heiress and medical student Muriel Gardiner. After the *Anschluss* in 1938, he and Gardiner fled to Paris, where they got married and helped Austrian Jews and Socialists escape the Nazis in Austria. In 1939, several months before the fall of France, the couple moved to the United States. Settling down in New York City, they kept helping many Austrian refugees with money and affidavits. Buttinger helped establish many of the refugee programs for the International Rescue Committee (IRC), helping to smuggle thousands of anti-Fascist refugees out of Europe. For over 40 years he served as director of the IRC's Paris office and European division, and as an IRC board member and vice president. In the 1950s, Buttinger published *In the Twilight of Socialism*, a critical history of Austrian Socialism in the years 1934-38. During the 1950s, he aided North Vietnamese refugees in South Vietnam and took an abiding interest in the history and culture of that country. He became a prominent scholar of Vietnamese history, producing a two-volume work entitled *Vietnam: A Dragon Embattled*. In 1972 the Chancellor of Austria, Bruno Kreisky, observed that "Mr. Buttinger was such a hero that if he had returned he would have become Chancellor" (Bischof, Buttinger).

Agnes and Alois Hebentodt

Agnes and Alois Hebentodt left Oberdrosen in Southern Burgenland for the U.S. in 1907. They were very poor and left their son Bruno behind with his grandparents. In the U.S. an additional seven kids were born (among them a son, Walter). Given the quota laws of 1924 and the worsening economic situation after the 1929 Great Depression, Bruno never made it to the U.S. Both Bruno and Walter were drafted respectively into their country's armies – Bruno into the German Wehrmacht and Walter joined the U.S. Navy. During the Normandy invasion of June 6, 1944, they fought on opposite sides, Bruno in the artillery, Walter in the Navy. Bruno ended up an American prisoner of war and was brought to a POW camp in Arizona, where his mother and "enemy" brother Walter visited him. His mother saw him for the first time in 40 years and the two brothers discovered that they had fought very close to each other on opposite sides on D-Day. Bruno returned to Burgenland after his one-year imprisonment in Arizona (*Burgenländische Germeinschaft*, January/February 1990, 5).

Rudolf Anzböck

Rudolf Anzböck, a young Viennese Socialist who was involved in sabotage action against Austrofascism and received the death sentence, had to flee Austria to save his life. One step ahead of the Nazis, Josef Buttinger, the leader of the Vienna "Revolutionary Socialists," managed to get him to New York from his Swedish exile. After a brief interlude in the 10th Mountain Division, the Office of Strategic Services' Labor Section recruited the Social Democrat. The wartime American intelligence organization OSS trained him and a number of Austrian compatriots for a "penetration" mission into Nazi Germany to gather intelligence on German and foreign slave laborers, and, if possible, unleash a revolt against the Nazis. But Anzböck never was dropped into Nazi Germany. Instead, he was used as a research analyst in London on assessing everyday life in Germany (pp. 222-261). The OSS decorated Anzböck for his service; he stayed involved in intelligence work after the war and, like most Austrian exiles, never returned to Austria. Traussnig makes a good case that many Austrian leftists like Anzböck continued their resistance against Austrofascism/Nazism from the prewar era into the wartime. Their personal contribution to the defeat of Hitlerism also contributed significantly to the "liberation of their former *Heimat*" (Traussnig, 222-61, 263).

For more information and multimedia content, visit the book's companion site at

www.austriainusa.org

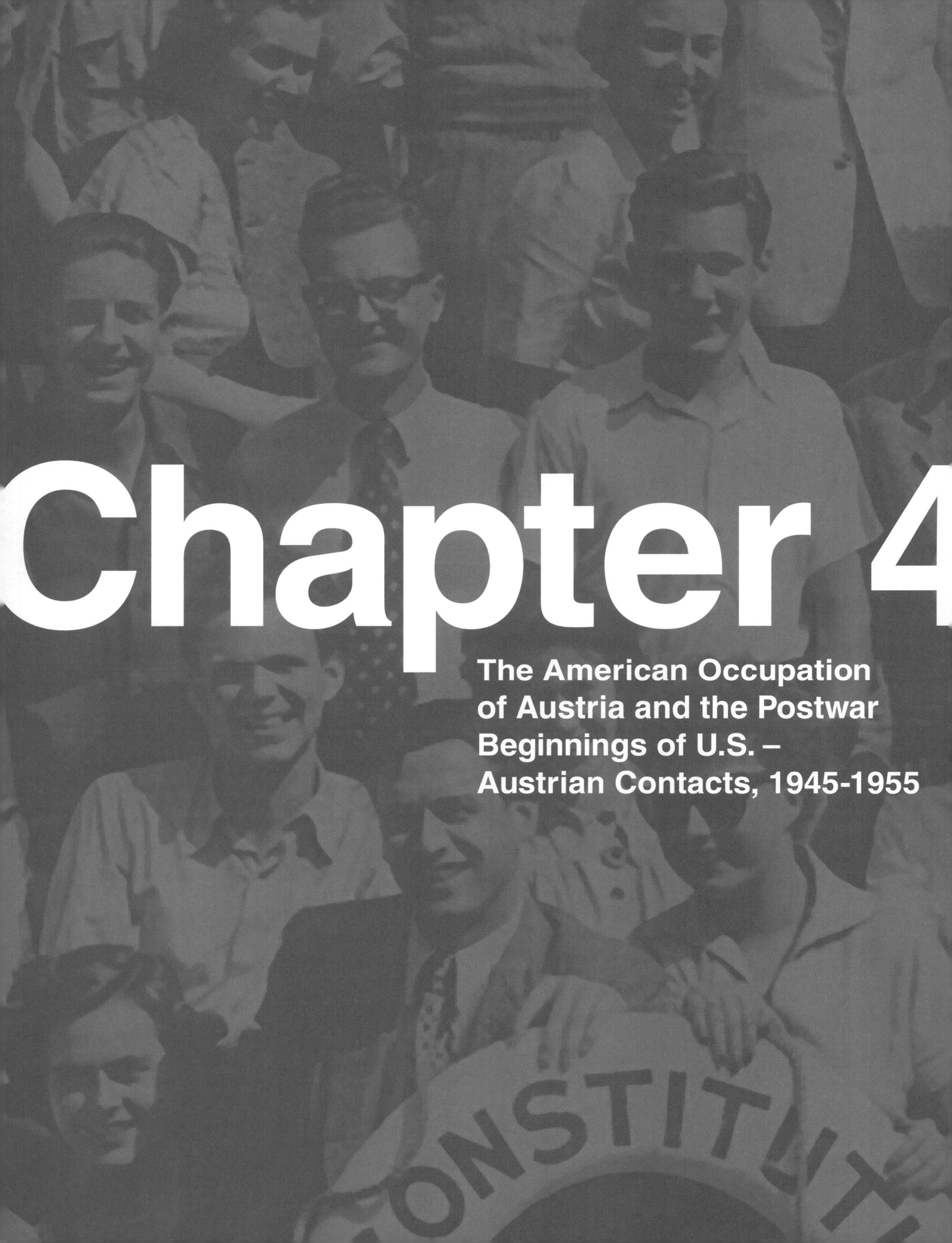

Chapter 4

The American Occupation
of Austria and the Postwar
Beginnings of U.S. –
Austrian Contacts, 1945-1955

Austrian – American bilateral relations never were as dense as during the four power occupation of Austria after World War II. While the victorious powers of World War II (United States, Great Britain, Soviet Union, and France) based on the 1943 "Moscow Declaration" treated Austria as a "liberated" country, they occupied Austria for ten years after the end of World War II as a result of growing Cold War tensions between the "free world" and the Communists. The powers considered Austria "the first victim" of Hitlerite aggression yet also reminded Austrians during the war that they needed to make a contribution to their own liberation. After a first wave of radical Denazification from 1945 to 1947 resulting in death sentences for a number of war criminals and the loss of political rights for former members of the Nazi party, the Austrian governments soon eagerly embraced their "victims" status so as not to pay reparations to the Allies and restitution to the Jews kicked out of the country after the *Anschluss* in 1938. Given its "liberated" status, the United States during the occupation funded both the survival of the Austrian population and the economic reconstruction of the country with aid programs such as the Marshall Plan. Both sides also initiated cultural programs to show to the other side the best face both countries had to offer. Student and faculty exchanges such as Fulbright and AFS were designed to impress and indoctrinate young visitors.

U.S. armed forces made a major contribution towards the liberation of Austria, where they feared Hitler would be making his "last stand" in his Alpine Fortress. The Third Division in General Patch's 7th Army liberated the city of Salzburg without much of a fight as the Nazi defenders retreated on May 4 without additional destruction of the city.

U.S. armed forces made a major contribution towards the liberation of Austria, where they feared Hitler would be making his "last stand" in his Alpine Fortress.

"Four in the Jeep" A symbol of the Allied occupation of post-War Vienna. The image shows an international military patrol in Vienna with the four representatives of the occupation powers leaning on the hood of the car, September 25, 1945.

During a Third Division commemorative ceremony at Arlington National Cemetery followed by a historic seminar at the Austrian Embassy in May 2015, the Mayor of Salzburg personally thanked the four 3rd Division veterans still alive and present at the event for their contribution to liberating Salzburg without destroying the city. At the same time American and French units chased towards the liberation of Hitler's "Eagle's Nest" in Berchtesgaden – a prestige prize for the conquerors. Units of the fabled American 101st airborne division liberated rural parts of Salzburg, including the city of Zell am See (American historian Stephen E. Ambrose has immortalized these events in his famous book *Band of Brothers*, later made into a Hollywood blockbuster TV series). General Patton's Third Army liberated Linz, the euthanasia center of Castle Hartheim, and the Concentration Camp of Mauthausen, encountering the full extent of Nazi atrocities committed on Austrian territory (Bischof in *Austrian Information* 68 (2015/16): 5-7).

In the final days of the war, the "monuments men" – a special team of art historians in the U.S. Army – secured huge treasure troves of art works stolen by the Nazis all over Europe. In a salt mine in Altausee, deep in the Austrian Alps, the monuments men discovered thousands of pictures designated for Hitler's *Führermuseum* in Linz, among them Jan Van Eyck's priceless Ghent Altarpieces. The story of the monuments men has recently been popularized in a Hollywood movie directed by and starring George Clooney. It stands to reason that much of the artistic heritage of the Western world was thus saved by a few American GIs.

When American GIs liberated Mauthausen KZ and its many subcamps (such as Ebensee) in early May, they first encountered the enormous depravity of the Nazi regime. Thousands of inmates, barely alive,

welcomed them and could not believe their good luck of seeing American soldiers who brought food. For many of the inmates the Americans had come too late; all that was left were piles of bodies of dead men. Meanwhile, General Patton sent a war crimes investigation team to Castle Hartheim under the leadership of Captain Charles Dameron from Port Allen, Louisiana.

In a salt mine in Altausee, deep in the Austrian Alps, the monuments men discovered thousands of pictures designated for Hitler's *Führermuseum* in Linz.

The Gent Altarpiece, discovered by the „monuments men" in a salt mine in Altausee in rural Salzburg.

Even before the fighting stopped in Austria, the Soviets set up the Provisional Renner Government in Vienna on April 27. The Anglo-American powers considered this government unilaterally established by Moscow as a "Soviet puppet" and did not recognize it; one third of the cabinet ministers were Communists.

Salzburg Arrival of U.S. Secretary for Agriculture Charles F. Brannan on the airfield of the United States Air Force. Dated July 26, 1951

General Geoffrey Keyes, who succeeded
General Mark Clark, delivers a Christmas
address on Austrian radio, recorded in the
Red-White-Red recording studio in Vienna
on December 24, 1949.

Salzburg General Clark delivers remarks at the opening ceremony of the Salzburg Festival, August 12, 1945. Seated (from the right) are Foreign Minister Gruber and soon to be Federal Chancellor Figl.

Establishing democratic institutions entailed the "denazification" of Austria. American occupation forces stayed in Austria during the early Cold War until the State Treaty was signed in 1955 as a means of providing security and contain the Communist threat to the new nation. General Geoffrey Keyes, Clark's successor advocated the rearmament of Austria after the Cold War intensified in 1948.

"The strategic importance of Austria [for the West] cannot be overemphasized."

In May/June 1945 Dameron's team interviewed local people and uncovered the full extent of Nazi euthanasia crimes, including the infamous "Hartheim Statistics." The Nazis had studiously documented the murder of some 70,000 handicapped and disabled Germans (18,000 Austrians in Hartheim) in the four major T-4 euthanasia killing centers in the Third Reich, Castle Hartheim being one of them.

Even before the fighting stopped in Austria, the Soviets set up the Provisional Renner Government in Vienna on April 27. The Anglo-American powers considered this government unilaterally established by Moscow as a "Soviet puppet" and did not recognize it; one third of the cabinet ministers were Communists. It would take another half year before the Western powers recognized the Renner Government and agreed to hold free elections in the late fall. The November 25 elections then brought a conservative-Socialist coalition government under Chancellor Leopold Figl into power (Bischof, *Leverage*, 42-51).

Yet under the first occupation agreement Austria was under the total tutelage of the occupation powers. Their most visible symbol of controlling Austria was the "Four in the Jeep" – soldiers of the four occupation powers policing the central first district of Vienna together in a Jeep. In June 1946 a Second Control Agreement was passed by the Allies that eased the control powers' tutelage of the country. Now the four powers could only stop constitutional laws passed by the Austrian parliament if they unanimously vetoed such laws. With the growing tensions in the Cold War such unanimous vetoes became unlikely. The Austrian government thus gained more control over its own affairs (Bischof, *Leverage*, 72-75).

The United States Forces in Austria, led by General Mark Clark who also served as High Commissioner, occupied their zone in Austria (Salzburg, Upper Austria south of the Danube) in May 1945, their sector in Vienna in August. In 1946, the U.S. had some 14,000 soldiers in Austria. Their mission was "to establish a free and independent Austria with a sound economy, capable of ensuring an adequate standard of living." Establishing democratic institutions entailed the "denazification" of Austria. American occupation forces stayed in Austria during the early Cold War until the State Treaty was signed in 1955 as a means of providing security and contain the Communist threat to the new nation. General Geoffrey Keyes, Clark's successor advocated the rearmament of Austria after the Cold War intensified in 1948. Like Messersmith before the war, he argued that "the strategic importance of Austria [for the West] cannot be overemphasized" (Bischof, *Leverage*, 113-19).

During the prolonged service in Austria, many GIs starved of female company during years of fighting on the frontlines, met Austrian women and fell in love with them. GIs were generous when they transitioned into becoming occupation soldiers and handed out candy to children and chocolates and silk stockings to women. Many married their girlfriends and brought them back to the United States even though the U.S. government made the immigration of "GI brides" difficult. Historians think ca. 4,000 to 5,000 Austrian girls married American GIs (1,200 from the American zone in Salzburg) and followed them to live in the U.S. (Maltschnig, *Austrian War Brides*, 229). With their marriages, quite a few of which broke up later, they also became Americans. In their Austrian home towns they met a lot of hostility going out with American servicemen (still seen by returning Wehrmacht soldiers as "the enemy"); locals called them "Ami whores." As one historian puts it – "there was no clear line between appetite for calories and appetite for life" (Maltschnig in Bischof, *Relationships*, 287-95).

Opening of the traveling exhibit "The Marshall Plan in the Tyrol," Kitzbühel, Austria, October 14, 1950.

Rebuilding after the wartime destruction and helping the Austrians establish a viable economy was the biggest challenge. American aid programs by the U.S. Army, private donations of CARE packages, UNRRA and Congressional relief programs fed Austrians and saved them from starvation. Almost one billion dollars of funds from the European Recovery Program ("Marshall Plan"), however, provided the biggest boost to rebuilding infrastructure and industries such as the Linz steel works, the paper & pulp and the textile industries, and modernize agriculture and tourism. Constructing the Kaprun power station high in the Alps was the largest project funded through ERP counterpart funds. By the early 1950s Austrians were no longer starving but were beginning to enjoy a higher standard of living in their daily lives (Bischof/Petschar).

The Marshall Plan still "lives on" in Austria. In 1961 the U.S. government transferred ca. one billion in "counterpart funds" to the Austrian government, which established the "*ERP-Fonds.*" This fund enjoys assets worth almost three billion Euros and is still providing investment funds for innovative projects to the Austrian economy today to the tune of 500 million Euros. The *ERP Fonds* set up the Austrian Marshall Plan Foundation in 2000 to organize student exchange programs with the U.S. (Bischof/Petschar, 258-309).

The Foreign Ministers of the four occupation powers (Dulles/US, Macmillan/GB, Pinay/France, Molotov/USSR) and Austrian Foreign Minister Leopold Figl signed the Austrian State Treaty on May 15, 1955, in Vienna's Belvedere Palace on a beautiful spring day. They presented the document to a large public assembled in the Belvedere gardens. Once the occupation soldiers had withdrawn from the country, the Austrian Parliament passed the neutrality law on October 26, 1955, restoring Austria's full sovereignty and defining its Cold War international status.

A tractor financed with Marshall Plan funds is being moved into the depot at the Heiligenstadt freight yard in Vienna, May 21, 1949.

Opening of the traveling exhibit "The Marshall Plan in the Tyrol."

Expansion of the water catchment system in the Mühlau district in Innsbruck, Austria, financed with Marshall Plan funds. February 25, 1953.

The new Soviet leadership under Khrushchev following Stalin's death in 1953, insisted on Austrian neutrality during bilateral meetings with the Raab government in early April 1955, as the final condition for evacuating the country (Bischof, *Leverage*, 142-49).

American diplomats, who had initiated the first treaty drafts in late 1945, consistently played a crucial role in negotiating the "Austrian Treaty" in some 400 meetings along with British, French, and Soviet diplomats. The Council of Foreign Ministers of the four powers held meetings in Moscow and London (1947), Paris (1949), and Berlin (1954) to work on the Austrian (and German) treaties. The Deputies of the Foreign Ministers met 260 times between 1947 and 1953 to work out the details of the 38 articles and 10 annexes of the treaty. A special Treaty Commission gathered in the summer of 1947 in 65 meetings to establish exact lists of "German assets" in Austria – the most vexing issue in the negotiations. Based on these lists, Austria paid $150 million to the Soviets out of current production to buy them out of Austria. Were it not for American Marshall Plan aid, the Austrian economy would not have been in good enough shape after 1955 to make these deliveries to Moscow. An Ambassadors Conference met in Vienna in late April/early May 1955 to put the final touches on the treaty before it was signed and ratified (Bischof, Cold War Miracle, in Bischof, *Relationships*, 153-64).

During the occupation a number of cultural programs were initiated between the U.S. and Austria. The exchange of students and scholars became a principal tool for promoting mutual understanding and influencing future elites. As early as 1945 what became known as the "European Forum" in Alpbach (a picturesque village in the Tyrolean Alps) attracted intellectuals from all over Europe and the U.S. It was set up by Austrians with

American funding. In 1947 Harvard students and faculty raised funds and organized the first gathering of European students at Castle Leopoldskron in Salzburg ("Salzburg Seminar"). Well-known Harvard faculty members such as F.O. Matthiesen and Daniel Aaron kept coming to Salzburg year after year to teach Europeans from East and West the basics of American civilization ("the intellectual Marshall Plan"). The "Salzburg Seminar" at the "Schloss" became a premier intellectual hub in Europe and also the birth place of "American Studies" on the continent. Both the "Alpbach Forum" and the "Salzburg Seminar" are still going strongly to this day (Bischof, Two Sides of the Coin, in: Bischof, *Relationships*, 41-43.)

On June 6, 1950 the Austrian and American governments signed the "Fulbright Agreement" establishing a joint "United States Educational Commission in Austria" and facilitating student and scholar exchanges. In 1951/52 the Fulbright program sent the first group of 139 Austrian students and faculty to American universities. By the year 2000 more than 3,100 Austrian "Fulbrighters" had come to the United States, while some 1,800 American scholars (students and faculty) came to Austria through the Fulbright program. The "American Field Service" (AFS) program began to send Austrian high school students to the U.S. in 1951/52. While by the 1960s five AFS students came to the U.S. annually, by the 1970s some 70 Austrian high school students came to the U.S. annually to live with American families and attend high schools (the author of these texts spent a year at San Ramon Valley High School in Danville, California, in 1972/73). Both Fulbright and AFS infused some 7,000 thousand young Austrians with a life-long enthusiasm for all things American (*Fulbright at 50; Austrian Information* 63 (Summer 2010); Bischof, Two Sides of the Coin, in: Bischof, *Relationships,* 38-40).

Opening of the traveling exhibit "The Marshall Plan in the Tyrol," locals inspecting statistical data. Kitzbühel, Austria, October 14, 1950.

Expansion of the water catchment system in the Mühlau district in Innsbruck, Austria, financed with Marshall Plan funds. February 25, 1953.

The Luttenberger Family celebrates their twelve year-old son's victory at a Marshall Plan drawing competition in Paris. Photograph taken in Feldbach, Austria, June 1951.

Signs announcing the extension of Federal Highway 181 in the state of Tyrol, financed with Marshall Plan funds, ca. 1955.

Austrian participants in a United States training program to increase productivity are on their way to being employed by U.S. companies for a year. The group is shown at Vienna's *Westbahnhof* train station on February 4, 1953.

The Austrian group at Vienna's Westbahnhof, on their way to the United States.

Construction of the Kaprun hydroelectric power plant dam 1954. The massive project, completed with Marshall Plan funds, yielded 815 million kilowatts of power when it opened after 15 years of construction. It was the largest project funded through ERP counterpart funds in Austria.

Kaprun Power Plant. Construction of dam wall (*Drossensperre*), partial view. November 16, 1953.

Presentation of a commemorative volume on the Marshall Plan in Vienna in 2017. From left: Eugene Young (Chargé d'affaires, Embassy of the United States in Austria), Federal President Alexander Van der Bellen, Vice Chancellor and Federal Minister of Justice Wolfgang Brandstetter, Professor Günter Bischof (The University of New Orleans), Dr. Hans Petschar (Austrian National Library), Virgil Widrich (filmmaker and producer), and Elisabeth Vogel (moderator, Austrian Broadcast Corporation).

Young Austrian leaders were brought on extended study trips to the U.S. through Marshall Plan and State Department visitor programs.

The Fulbright Program: Young Austrian scholar and Fulbright grantee portrayed before departure to the United States.

The Fulbright Program: Young Austrian scholar and Fulbright grantee portrayed before departure to the United States.

The Fulbright Program: Young Austrian scholar and Fulbright grantee portrayed before departure to the United States.

The Fulbright Program: Young Austrian scholar and Fulbright grantee portrayed before departure to the United States.

The Fulbright Program: Young Austrian scholar and Fulbright grantee portrayed before departure to the United States.

The first group of Austrian Fulbrighters on their way to the United States on the *USS Constitution*, 1951.

The first group of Austrian Fulbrighters on their way to the United States, photographed with their Captain aboard the *USS Constitution,* 1951.

Signing of the extension of the Fulbright Agreement between Austria and the United States in the Austrian Federal Chancellery, June 25, 1963. The signatories are J.W. Riddleberger, U.S. Ambassador to Austria (left) and Federal Minister for Foreign Affairs Bruno Kreisky.

U.S. Fulbright grantees arriving at Vienna's *Westbahnhof* train station in 1951.

In 1963, the famous Austrian émigré scholars Karl Lazarsfeld (a sociologist) and Oskar Morgenstern (an economist) helped found the "Institute for Advanced Studies" in Vienna (IHS – Institut für Höhere Studien). Financed by the Ford Foundation, American professors regularly came to Vienna to train young Austrian scholars in up-to-date social science methodologies. The cream of the crop of postwar Austrian political scientists such as Anton Pelinka and Peter Gerlich were trained at the IHS (Bischof, Two Sides of the Coin, in: Bischof, *Relationships*, 43; Pelinka). At the same time Austrian and American universities had developed bilateral partnership programs for the exchange of students and faculty such as the activities between the Universities of New Orleans and Innsbruck, Emory University and the University of Vienna, or the University of Illinois at Urbana-Champaign and the Wirtschaftsuniversität Wien. As early as 1962 Wagner College of Staten Island, New York City, was one of the first private colleges to initiate a year-long program for some 80 students annually in Bregenz.

Culturally, both Austria and the United States built long-lasting ties and programs between themselves. During the American occupation of Austria (1945-55), the U.S. established a strong cultural presence with its "America Houses" in Austria. Austrians enjoyed visiting the reading rooms in the America Houses in Vienna, Linz, and Salzburg, which provided books (including the ones that had previously been prohibited by the Nazis), magazines, and newspapers. During the Marshall Plan era, American "book mobiles" came into the most remote Alpine corners of Austria to provide access to reading materials. Young people came to appreciate American popular culture from Jeans to Coca Cola and Jazz music. The U.S. supported "American Studies" programs and thus brought the serious study of America to Austrian universities.

A sign greeting guests of the European Forum Alpbach, ca. 1950. The sign reads "European Forum Alpbach – The Austrian College Greets its Guests."

Opening of the European Forum Alpbach, August 24, 1952.

Opening of the European Forum Alpbach with the Alpbach Brass Band, August 24, 1952.

State Department cultural officers also brought "high brow" American culture to Austrians – from George Gershwin's opera "Porgy and Bess" to the plays of Thornton Wilder and Arthur Miller. Young Austrian leaders were brought on extended study trips to the U.S. through Marshall Plan and State Department visitor programs. Scholars have called this entire process "the Coca-colonization"/Americanization of Austria (*Wagnleitner*).

During World War II Austrian émigrés started Austrian organizations to promote Austrian identity and culture, as well as fighting for postwar Austrian independence – the Austrian Institute as early as 1942, as well as the Austrian Cultural Forum in New York. Out of these wartime émigré institutions the Austrian cultural presence in postwar America emerged. After the war the Austria Institute was incorporated in 1947 and put its focus on promoting Austrian culture in the U.S. In 1948 the Austrian government established the Austrian Information Service in New York. Fritz Molden, a resistance fighter during World War II who launched a career as a journalist after the war, served as its first director in its offices on 5th Avenue and 42nd Street. The Information Service was also tasked with reaching out to victims of the Holocaust and Austrian émigrés forced to leave the country in 1938. In 1992 the Austrian Information Service (henceforth known as the *Austrian Press and Information Service*) relocated to the Embassy in Washington, DC and its newly errected chancery building (*Austrian Information* 3/13 (2018)).

In 1963 the Education Ministry opened the Austrian Cultural Institute in New York on 11 East 52nd Street as a clearing house for all things Austrian in the vast metropolis with its large Austrian émigré community. On Chancellor Bruno Kreisky's insistence in 1973, the Cultural Institute and the Information Service were integrated into the Foreign Ministry.

International Seminar at Leopoldskron Castle,
Salzburg, August 18, 1949.

International Seminar at Leopoldskron Castle, Salzburg, August 18, 1949.

International Seminar at Leopoldskron Castle, Salzburg, August 18, 1949.

International Seminar on American Culture at
Leopoldskron Castle, Salzburg, February 14, 1951.

Paul Lazarsfeld

Emigré scholars Paul Lazarsfeld and Oskar Morgenstern were instrumental in the formation of the *Institute of Advanced Studies* in Vienna.

Oskar Morgenstern

Emigré scholars Paul Lazarsfeld and Oskar Morgenstern were instrumental in the formation of the *Institute of Advanced Studies* in Vienna.

The journalist, publicist and diplomat Fritz Molden shown here in ca. 1975, was the inaugural director of the Austrian Information Service in New York City. Molden married Joan Dulles, daughter of Allen Welsh Dulles, in 1948.

Farewell ceremony for the Cultural Advisor of the Austrian Federal Ministry of Education in New York, Wilhelm Schlag, before his departure on December 16, 1955. From left: Ambassador of the United States to Austria Llewellyn E. Thompson, Foreign Minister Leopold Figl, Samuel H. Linch and Wilhelm Schlag.

Raimund Abraham's narrow skyscraper on 52nd Street, a Manhattan landmark, has been home to the Austrian Cultural Forum New York since 2002. The building is designed to express the contextual relevance of both the architecture and the Forum's mission to connect European and American creative visions.

Christoph Thun-Hohenstein (left) and architect Raimund Abraham at the new building of the Austrian Cultural Forum in New York City, 2002.

These student exchanges and private initiatives have succeeded as much as official relations in maintaining stable contacts between the two countries on a broad basis.

Even though its members were getting older, the Austrian Cultural Forum still existed and organized cultural programs (especially musical performances), many of them on the premises of the new Cultural Institute. Wilhelm Schlag was the founding director and served for the first ten years as the impresario of the Austrian cultural presence in the United States. He first learned about the U.S. as a prisoner of war in the Midwest; he became the first general secretary of the Austrian Fulbright Commission, and the Austrian government first dispatched him to the U.S. as Austria's cultural representative in 1956. Schlag fully integrated the Jewish émigrés' Cultural Forum activities into the Austrian Institute. The émigré writer Mimi Grossberg helped him develop a literature program (Seidl, 132-33). Peter Marboe and Wolfgang Waldner directed the Cultural Institute through the 1980s and 1990s. Waldner suggested a new building on the site of the Cultural Institute on 52nd Street and organized an architectural contest, which Austrian architect Raimund Abraham won with a surreal looking plan for the small site. In 2001 the Cultural Institute was renamed the Austrian Cultural Forum; in 2007, it moved into the spectacular new building on 11 East 52nd Street – now an architectural landmark in New York City, where contemporary Austrian arts and culture are regularly on display (Seidl, 202-209).

The Austrian Cultural Institute/Forum has had a strong presence in New York City but less so in the rest of the country. Private initiatives and university partnerships have been picking up the slack. After World War II the Trapp Family Singers (immortalized in the Hollywood hit movie *The Sound of Music*) probably have done more to promote the image of Austria in the U.S. than official representatives. In 1976 the government of Bruno Kreisky donated two Austrian chairs to American universities as an Austrian bicentennial gift (raised by public donations), one at the University of Minnesota-Twin Cities and the other at Stanford University. The Center for Austrian Studies at the University in Minnesota has been promoting the study of Austria ever since. Since 1976 the University of New Orleans has been sending students from Southern universities to Innsbruck – more than 10,000 since its inception. In 1997 the University of New Orleans initiated *Center Austria* (today the Austrian Marshall Plan Center for European Studies) to build additional contacts with its partner university in Innsbruck. Meanwhile dozens of American universities maintain study programs in Austria and Austrian universities regularly send students to the United States. Since 2000 the Austrian Marshall Plan Foundation has built programs with the University of New Orleans, the University of California, Berkeley, and Johns Hopkins University's *School of Advanced International Studies (SAIS)* in Washington, DC. Since 2008 the Botstiber Foundation of Media, Pennsylvania, with its Institute of Austrian-American Studies and its new *Journal of Austrian-American History* has been generously funding and promoting Austrian Studies in the United States. These student exchanges and private initiatives have succeeded as much as official relations in maintaining stable contacts between the two countries on a broad basis.

The Austrian Marshall Plan Center for European Studies at The University of New Orleans celebrated 20 years in 2017 with a proper *second line* parade in New Orleans' French Quarter. Academic cooperation between New Orleans and its Austrian Sister City Innsbruck dates back to the 1970s.

Dietrich W. Botstiber
(1912 - 2002)

Dietrich grew up in a Vienna environment of high culture and the arts; his Catholic mother was an alto opera singer – his Jewish-Hungarian father was one of Vienna's premier music managers, directing the *Wiener Konzerthaus* for many years. Peter Drucker, who also emigrated to the U.S. and became America's premier management guru, was his best childhood friend. Against his father's wishes he studied mechanical and electrical engineering at Vienna's famed Technical University. As he put it in his memoirs *Not on the Mayflower:* "To my father, the world, or its purpose, consisted of music, culture, the arts, their masters, their history, and their development. Unfortunately, his son was a barbarian who was obsessed with industry, engines, airplanes – and America" (Botstiber, 164). As early as 1931 he was beginning to plan to emigrate to the United States, where opportunities were better; in 1938 he finally received his visa and left for New York (while his parents left for England). Settling in Philadelphia, he first worked as an electrician before he quickly moved up in an engineering career, culminating in his naturalization in 1943. In 1947 he began working for the *Piasecki Helicopter Corporation* and became its chief engineer only four years later. In 1952 he launched his own business, the *Technical Development Company (TEDECO)*, which developed and manufactured aircraft engine accessories. In 1985 he sold his company, which by then was employing 235 people and totalling annual sales of $20 million. Botstiber left his fortune for philanthropic work and the Botstiber Foundation was set up. In 2008 the Foundation set up the Botstiber Institute for Austrian-American Studies. It has become a premier institution funding and promoting Austrian Studies in the United States. Dietrich Botstiber thus has left a lasting legacy in strengthening Austrian-American relations for a long time to come (Lackner in Bischof, 183-96; Botstiber in JAAH, 1-39).

Irene Harand (1900 -1975)

Irene Harand was an early Austrian campaigner against antisemitism after the rise of Hitler. Born a Roman Catholic in Vienna, Harand was an early organizer of protests against Nazi Germany's persecutions of Jews. She started the movement *Weltbewegung gegen Rassenhass und Menschennot* [World Movement Against Racial Hatred and Human Suffering] in 1933 and actively campaigned throughout Europe before World War II. Though not opposed to the Austrofascist rule of Engelbert Dollfuss, Harand was a courageous fighter against antisemitic sentiments and Nazism. To counter Adolf Hitler's autobiographical text *Mein Kampf*, she wrote a book named *Sein Kampf - Antwort an Hitler von Irene Harand* [His Struggle - the Answer to Hitler from Irene Harand]. When Nazi Germany invaded and annexed Austria to the Third Reich in 1938, Harand happened to be lecturing in London; it saved her life as the Nazis had set a price for her capture. She emigrated to the United States, where she was involved in establishing the Austrian Forum; after the war it became the basis for the Austrian Cultural Forum. In 1963 she became its leader. In 1969 she received the honorary title of a "Righteous among the Nations" from the state of Israel for her resistance against Nazi anti-Semitism. Harand died in New York in 1975, but was buried in Vienna. In 2008 a square in the Vienna district of Wieden was named in her honor (Seidl, 44).

Erna H. (1933-)

Erna H. was born in Leogang, Salzburg, as an illegitimate child. She had a bad relationship with her "substitute mother." She returned to the city of Salzburg after longish stays in Switzerland and in England. She married the American GI Cliff, whom she had met at her mother's place, after a year of courtship. Erna was introduced to Cliff by her mother, who had been washing Cliff's clothes. Cliff brought Erna to the U.S. after their marriage. Cliff's family was not too enthusiastic about him marrying a "foreigner" and bringing her back to the U.S. "Why did you have to marry her?" asked Cliff's dad. Cliff stayed in the army and the family moved around a lot with Erna raising five sons, often at home by herself during Cliff's long absences (like his tours in the Vietnam War). In the mid-1960s she and her family finally settled down in Georgia. Erna was a homemaker and never worked outside her home. Erna claims her life in the U.S. boosted her self-esteem. She learned how to be independent and speak her mind – she is "still writing the checks" in the family. She revisited Austria for the first time in 1995. (Eva Maltschnig Interview with Erna H., Dec. 2011, in: Maltschnig in Bischof, 291-92).

Fo
inf
an
mu
co

more

rmation

ltimedia

ntent,

visit the book's companion
site at www.austriainusa.org

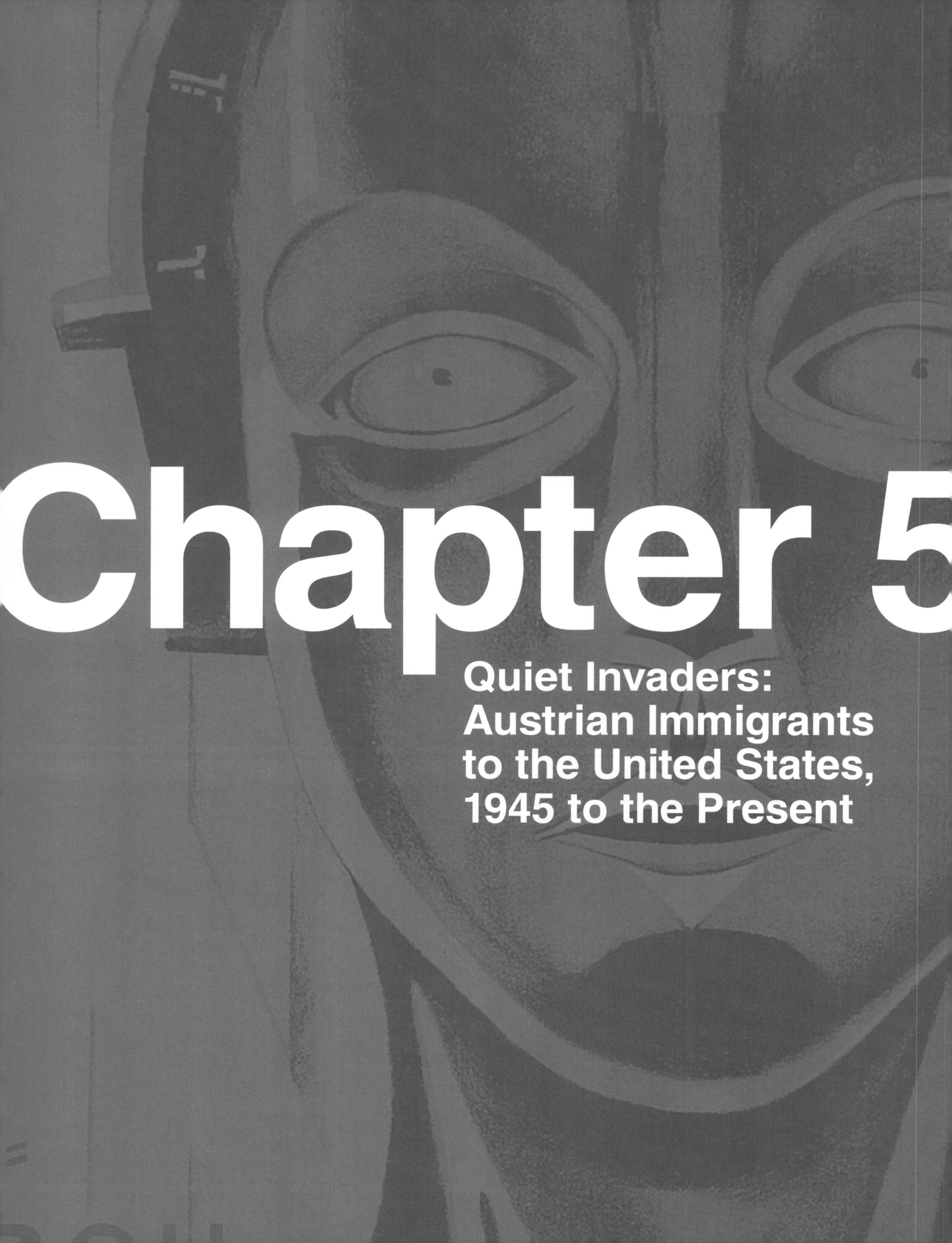

Chapter 5

Quiet Invaders:
Austrian Immigrants
to the United States,
1945 to the Present

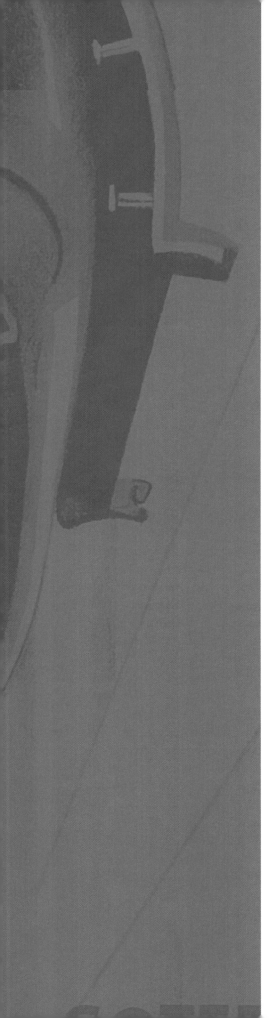

Migrants from Austria kept coming to the United States after World War II and are coming to this day. Looking for better economic opportunities after the war and better professional chances today have remained the principal attraction of the U.S. after World War II. At the end of World War II, more than 1,5 million Displaced Persons (DPs) were stranded in Austrian camps. They were not admitted under the regular quota laws of 1921/24 but immigration laws needed to be changed to admit these desperate refugees (ethnic Germans, Jews, people from the Baltic states etc.), most of them displaced by Hitler's war of aggression in Eastern Europe. Between 1945 and 1952, some 450,000 refugee DPs were admitted to the U.S. on special immigration legislation passed by Congress. During crises in the Soviet Bloc (Hungary 1956, Czechoslovakia 1968, Poland 1980/81) tens of thousands of refugees from these crises regions got stranded on Austrian soil across the Iron Curtain – the U.S. admitted thousands of these refugees under emergency piecemeal immigration registration. The United States Congress passed an Immigration Law in 1965, ending the racist national origins quota system of 1924. Family reunions and professionals of exceptional ability were the new categories. As a result hundreds of thousands of Asians and Latin Americans entered the country, while the flow of Europeans slowed down to a trickle as a result of the postwar economic boom in Europe (Daniels, 328-44). Whereas in the 1950s half of all the immigrants to the U.S. came from Europe, by the 1960s it was a third, and by the 1980s Europeans represented only 10 percent of the legal immigrant population (Daniels, 33). From 1945 until 1960 about 40,000 Austrians immigrated to the U.S. – with the annual quota for Austria being ca. 1,400. In spite of the 1965 immigration law abandoning quotas – and with the postwar Austrian economic boom making migration less attractive, only about

20,000 Austrians came to the U.S. between 1966 and 1975 (of which only some 8,000 listed Austria as their place of birth) (Luebke, *Austrians*, 169). From 1990 to 1999, 18,234 Austrians obtained legal resident status in the U.S. While in 1999, 230 Austrians were naturalized as U.S. citizens, in 2007 it was 292.

HOLLYWOOD

Migrants from "old" Habsburg Austria and "new" Republican Austria left a remarkable imprint on the Hollywood film industry. Directors, producers, actors, agents, composers of film music all made vital contributions to the "most American" art form – film. Many began in entertainment and theaters in Vienna and Berlin and moved on to film – switching from theater being based on language to film dedicated to image. Some came before World War I, most after the war – a flood of Jewish artists in the 1930s. Directors such a Fritz Lang, Otto Preminger, Max Reinhard, Fred Zinneman, Josef von Sternberg, Berthold Viertel, and Edgar Ulmer, all born in Vienna, put their imprint on Hollywood before and after World War II. Samuel "Billy" Wilder was born in Sucha, Galicia, in the Habsburg Monarchy and came to Hollywood via Vienna, Berlin, and Paris. Wilder knew what the ascent of Hitler meant to Jews: "I was on the train to Paris the day after the Reichstag fire." Wilder became successful during World War II as a screen writer and director, making "film noirs" and after the war increasingly focused on comedies such as *The Apartment* (1960), which won three Oscars in 1960 (Best Movie, Best Director, Best Screenplay), after having won three Oscars previously; altogether Wilder received a record 21 Academy Award nominations.

Vienna-born migrants such as Hans Julius Salter and Max Steiner, Brno-born Erich Wolfgang Korngold, along with Hanns Eisler (of Viennese parentage) were among the most successful composers of film music in Hollywood and infused American film with the "Vienna touch." They all received Academy Award nominations, Korngold won two Oscars for best film music (*Adventures of Robin Hood*, 1938). Korngold imagined the film music score "as an opera without singing." The Communist Eisler was forced to return to Europe after the House Un-American Activities Committee investigated him in the late 1940s ("McCarthyism"). Bohemian-born Paul Kohner, one of three brothers who went into the film business, started the most famous agency in Hollywood, helping numerous Europeans to get visas and find work in Hollywood during and after World War II. Vienna-born Ilse Lahn worked in his agency as a script-reader. Numerous actors became Hollywood stars after their stage careers in Vienna. Theodor Bikel starred with Humphrey Bogart (winning his only Oscar for best actor) and Katherine Hepburn in director John Huston's and producer Sam Spiegel's *African Queen* (1951), and later as the milkman Tevje in *Fiddler on the Roof* (1969). Vienna-born Hedy Lamarr advanced to stardom in Metro-Goldwyn-Mayer, often typecast as the archetypal glamorous seductress of exotic origin, elevating her to a sex symbol for American soldiers during World War II. She starred in 30 films. Self-taught, she also became an inventor. Among other inventions, she developed frequency-hopping signals for torpedoes so they could not be tracked or jammed. The U.S. Navy only adopted her technology in 1962. Her work on spread spectrum technology contributed to the development of *Bluetooth*, and Wi-Fi. Married six times, she died in seclusion. More recently Arnold Schwarzenegger and Christoph Waltz have seen success in Hollywood – Waltz winning two Oscars.

Migrants from "old" Habsburg Austria and "new" Republican Austria left a remarkable imprint on the Hollywood film industry. Directors, producers, actors, agents, composers of film music all made vital contributions to the "most American" art form – film. Many began in entertainment and theaters in Vienna and Berlin and moved on to film – switching from theater being based on language to film dedicated to image.

Fritz Lang (1890 - 1976) Fritz Lang (photographed here in 1971) was born in Vienna, Austria-Hungary in 1890 and is regarded among the most influential filmmakers of the expressionist movement, which was building during the early 20th century, particularly in Berlin, Germany, where Lang worked before emigrating. He left Germany in 1933 for Paris before settling in the United States. Lang is best known for the groundbreaking *Metropolis* (1927) and *M* (1931). Once in Hollywood, he made substantial contributions to American genre cinema, specifically *film noir*.

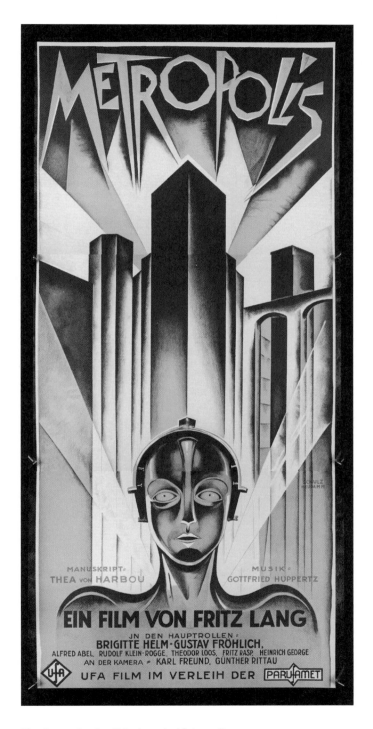

Movie poster for Fritz Lang's *Metropolis.*

Josef von Sternberg (1894 – 1969) *Director, Cinematographer* Born in Vienna, Austria-Hungary in 1894, Josef von Sternberg moved to the United States with his family in 1901 at the age of seven. Besides his reputation for camera work, pictorial composition and eye for décor, Sternberg is well known for his work with Marlene Dietrich, which would develop into one of Hollywood's legendary partnerships.

It gave birth to iconic films including *The Blue Angel* (1930), *Morocco* (1930), or *Shanghai Express* (1932), among many others. In addition, Sternberg has also been credited with creating the gangster film genre through *Underworld* (1927). Sternberg was nominated for Academy Awards for Best Director for *Morocco and Shanghai Express.*

Erich von Stroheim (1885 – 1957) *Director* Erich von Stroheim was born in Vienna, Austria-Hungary in 1885 and immigrated to the United States in 1909. He is regarded as a visionary director of the silent film era. Specifically, the 1924 silent *Greed* today is considered one of the greatest films ever made. Stroheim was banned from Hollywood for life after clashing with studios over several issues, including workers' rights. He subsequently continued his career as a respected character actor in France, where he passed away in 1957.

Max Steiner (1888 – 1971) *Composer* Max Steiner was born in 1888 in Vienna, Austria-Hungary and moved to Hollywood in 1929. He was one of the first composers of film music scores. He composed over 300 scores, ranging from iconic films like *King Kong* to *Gone with the Wind* and *Casablanca*. Over the course of his career, Steiner was nominated for 24 *Academy Awards* and won three - for *The Informer* (1935), *Now, Voyager* (1942), and *Since You Went Away* (1944). In addition, Steiner also won the first Golden Globe for Best Original Score.

Erich Wolfgang Korngold (1897 – 1957) *Composer* Erich Wolfgang Korngold was one of the most influential composers in Hollywood history. Along with Alfred Newman and Max Steiner, he is considered to be a founder of film music. Korngold moved to the United States in 1934 and began composing for Hollywood films. He won *Academy Awards* for Best Original Music Score for *Anthony Adverse* (1936) and *The Adventures of Robin Hood* (1938). Born on May 29, 1897 in Brünn (Brno), Austria-Hungary, he became a child prodigy in Vienna, where Gustav Mahler called him a "musical genius."

Sam Spiegel (1901 – 1985) *Producer* Sam Spiegel
was born in Jaroslaw, Austrian Poland in 1901. After
attending the University of Vienna, he immigrated
to the United States in 1938 via Mexico. Spiegel,
a producer, was the first to win Academy Awards
for Best Picture three times, for *On the Waterfront*
(1954), *The Bridge on the River Kwai* (1957), and
Lawrence of Arabia (1962). Other well-known films
produced by Spiegel include *The African Queen*
(1951) and *The Last Tycoon* (1976). Spiegel (right)
is depicted here with Olivia de Havilland and David
Lean at the 35th Academy Awards in 1963. Both
Spiegel and Lean received Academy Awards for
Lawrence of Arabia that night.

Johnny Weissmuller (1904 – 1984) *Swimmer, Actor* Jonny Weissmuller
was born in Freidorf, Austria-Hungary (present-day Timisoara, Romania)
in 1904. Before his acting career, Weissmuller was one of the world's
top competitive swimmers; he won five Olympic gold medals and was
also the first human to swim 100 meters in under a minute. In addition,
Weissmuller also won over 50 United States championships and set over
50 world records. Weissmuller arrived in New York on the *SS Rotterdam*.
He achieved Hollywood fame through his portrayal of Tarzan in *Tarzan the
Ape Man* (1932), which propelled him to international stardom. He starred
in several more Tarzan movies before switching to the role of *Jungle Jim*
(1948) in 13 movies.

Weissmuller is pictured here arriving at Schiphol Airport, Amsterdam, on June 24, 1970.

Peter Lorre (1904 – 1964) *Actor* Peter Lorre was born László Löwenstein in Rosenberg, Austria-Hungary (present-day Slovakia) in 1904. After enjoying a stage career in Vienna and Berlin, Lorre received international attention for his portrayal of a serial killer in Fritz Lang's *M* (1931). Lorre eventually settled in Hollywood.

Movie poster for Alfred Hitchcock's *The Man Who Knew Too Much*, **starring**
Peter Lorre (1934).

Fred Zinnemann (1907 – 1997) *Director* Alfred Zinnemann was born in Resche, Austria-Hungary
(Rzeszów in present-day Poland) in 1907 to a family of Austrian Jews. Both his parents perished
in the Holocaust. Zinnemann first arrived in New York City in 1929 before moving to Hollywood.
There, he directed 25 feature films, including some of Hollywood's biggest, including *From Here to
Eternity (*1953), *Oklahoma!* (1955), as well as *The Day of the Jackal* (1973), and *Julia* (1977). He
debuted a number of stars, including Marlon Brando, Rod Steiger, and Meryl Streep. Zinnemann's
films received a total of 65 Academy Award nominations and were awarded 24. Zinnemann himself
won four Academy Awards, for Best Short Subject for *That Mothers Might Live* (1938), for Best
Documentary Short Subject for *Benjy* (1951), for Best Director for *From Here to Eternity* (1953)
and for *A Man for All Seasons (*1966).

Hedy Lamarr (1914 – 2000) *Actress* Hedy Lamarr was born Hedwig Eva Maria Kiesler on November 9, 1914 in Vienna, Austria-Hungary. She arrived in Hollywood via London in 1937. Initially famous for her striking beauty and Hollywood stardom, Lamarr was also a self-taught inventor. With composer George Antheil, she developed a spread-spectrum, "frequency hopping" technology, which is widely used in telecommunications and can be found in *Bluetooth, Wifi,* and other technologies. Only more recently did her substantial contributions to modern technology receive proper recognition. In 2014 Lamarr and Antheil were posthumously inducted into the National Inventors Hall of Fame.

Billy Wilder (1906 - 2002) *Director* Billy Wilder
was one of the defining filmmakers of Hollywood's
Golden Age. Wilder was born on June 22, 1906
into an Austrian Jewish family in Sucha Beskidzka,
Austria-Hungary. He moved to Hollywood via
Paris in 1933. Members of his immediate family
perished in the Holocaust. In the United States,
Billy Wilder reached Hollywood superstardom
with films including *Sunset Boulevard (*1950),
Some Like It Hot (1959), or *The Apartment* (1960).
During his career spanning over five decades,
Billy Wilder received 21 Academy Award
nominations and won a total of six Oscars. He
was the first person to win Academy Awards as
director, producer and screenwriter for the same
film *(The Apartment).*

Otto Preminger (1905 – 1986) *Director* Otto Preminger is noted for his contributions to film noir in America as a stage and film director. In addition, he is also credited with moving the boundaries of censorship in movies by introducing taboo topics, including the 1959 *Anatomy of a Murder* (thematising rape). He was nominated twice for the Academy Award for Best Director. Preminger was born in Wisnitz, Austria-Hungary (in present-day Ukraine) in 1905.

Harry Horner (1910 – 1994) *Art Director* Harry Horner was born in Holitz, Austria-Hungary in 1910 (present-day Czech Republic). A contemporary of Max Reinhardt, Horner followed him to the United States as stage manager. As an art director, Horner won two Academy Awards for Best Production Design for *The Heiress (*1949) and *The Hustler* (1961) and was nominated a third time for *They Shoot Horses, Don't They?* (1969). Horner also worked as a director in both film and in television, including the well-known Western drama *Gunsmoke* (1952 – 1961). Shown above is a movie poster for *Red Planet Mars* (1952), directed by Horner.

Curd Jürgens (1915 – 1971) *Actor* Curd Jürgens, born in Solln, Germany, never formally immigrated to the United States, but has left an imprint on Hollywood through his work in many productions. His first Hollywood feature was *The Enemy Below* (1957), he went on to portray General Günther Blumentritt in the epic war film *The Longest Day* (1962). In addition, Jürgens is also known to audiences worldwide through his portrayal of bond villain Karl Stromberg in *The Spy Who Loved Me* (1977). Jürgens, who had always considered himself a stage actor, appeared in over 100 films. He is pictured here at a book signing in Kiel, Germany on October 10, 1976.

Maximilian Schell (1930 – 2014) *Actor* Maximillian Schell was born in Vienna, Austria in 1930 (as a Swiss citizen), and while he never formally immigrated to the United States, he did leave a substantial imprint on Hollywood. Schell won the Academy Award for Best Actor for his work in *Judgment at Nuremberg* (1961) – the first for a German-speaking actor since World War II. In addition, he received two more Academy Award nominations, for Best Actor in *The Man in the Glass Booth* (1975) and for Best Supporting Actor in *Julia (*1977).Schell also served as a guest professor at the University of Southern California and produced a number of operas. He passed away in Innsbruck, Austria in 2014.

Klaus Maria Brandauer *Actor, Director* Klaus Maria Brandauer, born in Bad Aussee, Austria in 1943, rose to fame internationally through his work in *Mephisto* (1981), a Hungarian production, before portraying Bond villain and Sean Connery's opponent Maximilian Largo in *Never Say Never Again* (1983). Brandauer subsequently starred with Meryl Streep and Robert Redford in *Out of Africa (*1985), a performance that won him a Golden Globe and an Academy Award nomination. Brandauer would eventually work with Sean Connery again in the spy film *The Russia House* (1990). He is pictured here with Sean Connery in 1982.

Arnold Schwarzenegger *Actor* Arnold Schwarzenegger was born on July 30, 1947 in Thal (close to Graz), Austria. With only a few dollars in his pocket, he immigrated to the United States in 1968 at the age of 21 to pursue his bodybuilding career. Over the years, Schwarzenegger became one of the defining figures in bodybuilding and built an acting career culminating in numerous box office hits, including the *Terminator* franchise. Also pursuing a political career, Schwarzenegger served as the 38th Governor of California from 2003 until 2011.

Christoph Waltz *Actor* Christoph Waltz, born
into an Austrian-German theater family in Vienna,
Austria in 1956, is best known in the United
States through his work with director Quentin
Tarantino. He received acclaim for his portrayals
of Hans Landa in *Inglorious Basterds* (2009) and
Dr. King Schultz in *Django Unchained* (2012).
He won Academy Awards for both performances
and subsequently also portrayed James Bond's
nemesis Ernst Stavro Blofeld in *Spectre* (2015).
Christoph Waltz today lives in Berlin, London,
and Los Angeles. He is depicted here next to
co-star Jamie Foxx in Quentin Tarrantino's
Django Unchained (2012).

Mall Man: Victor Gruen has been widely regarded as the father and architect of an icon of modern American life: the shopping mall. Born in Vienna in 1903 as David Victor Grünbaum to a Jewish family, he was forced to leave his native Austria in 1938 and eventually settled in the United States. With his California-based firm, *Victor Gruen Associates*, he conceptualized and built the first modern shopping malls in the country, eventually transforming the American (sub)urban landscape.

THE ARCHITECTS

The exodus of top Austrian talent to the United States reached a flood-state with the expulsion of Jews after the *Anschluss*. Among many "modernist" architects leaving for the U.S., Victor Gruen (*neé* David Victor Grünbaum), Richard Neutra, Rudolf M. Schindler, and Frederick Kiesler were among the best known. Gruen built the first shopping malls in the United States. *Northland* opened its doors in Southfield, Michigan, in 1954. Gruen tried to arrest the social isolation created by suburbanization and sprawl after World War II with the communal and interactive urban environment he had experienced growing up in Vienna. World famous fin de siècle Vienna architect Adolf Loos kindled Neutra's interest in urban America. Frank Lloyd Wright became his American mentor and his Vienna classmate Schindler invited him to come to Los Angeles. Neutra's architectural *biorealism* style was influenced by Freud's psychoanalysis. He became famous for his single family homes, whose designs aimed at being an extension of the nature of their owners. *The Lovell House* (1929) in Los Angeles became his best known creation. Schindler built a house for himself in the early 1920s. After its purchase by the Austrian government in 1995, it has become the Austrian Museum of Applied Arts (MAK) Center for Art and Architecture in Los Angeles – carrying on Schindler's modernist tradition as a forum for cultural and artistic exchanges by designers, artists, and architects. Frederick Kiesler started designs for an *endless house*, collapsing the boundaries between art and architecture. Radically re-envisioning the possibilities of dwelling, Kiesler wrote that "the house must be a cosmos in itself, a transformer of life-forces." He was also one of the architects of the famous *Shrine of the Book*, part of the Israel Museum in Jerusalem.

"**I am often called the father of the shopping mall. I would like to take this opportunity to disclaim paternity once and for all. I refuse to pay alimony to those bastard developments. They destroyed our cities.**"

- Victor Gruen, 1975

For Gruen, the design of shopping malls always went hand in hand with a desire to create communal places that go beyond consumerism and enhance the quality of life.

He became increasingly disappointed with the direction subsequent developments took and distanced himself – the shopping mall had diverged from his original vision.

Victor Gruen. Northland Center, Southfield, Michigan Northland Center, outside Detroit, Michigan opened in 1954. It was a milestone development and the largest completely integrated retail shopping district in the world. According to Gruen Associates, emphasis was placed on the long range development of the shopping center and the creation of a desirable public urban space.

Northland was demolished for redevelopment. The last anchor store closed in 2015, and demolition began in 2017.

Victor Gruen. Southdale Center, Edina, Minnesota In 1956, Gruen designed the first climate-controlled, all-enclosed shopping center in the world – Southdale Center in Edina, Minnesota. It was recognized as one of the ten most influential buildings in the United States. Victor Gruen envisioned the enclosed regional shopping mall as livable spaces that encourage people to get out of their cars and interact with each other. The mall still operates today.

Victor Gruen. Southdale Center, Edina, Minnesota

Victor Gruen. Southdale Center, Edina, Minnesota.

California Modernist: Richard Neutra (1892-1970) "What will the neighbors think?" asked *Time*, who featured Neutra on the cover of the August 15, 1949 issue. Richard Joseph Neutra is widely considered one of the most influential modernist architects. Born in Vienna on April 8, 1882, he moved to the United States in 1923, where he first worked with Frank Lloyd Wright and fellow Austrian Rudolf Schindler.

"Neutra emphasizes the "ready for anything" plan – stressing an open, multifunctional plan for living spaces that are flexible, adaptable and easily modified for any type of life or event."

- Los Angeles Times, 1947

Richard Neutra. Mariner's Medical Building,
Newport Beach, California.

Richard Neutra. Gettysburg Visitors Center, Cyclorama Building (demolished in 2013).

Richard Neutra. Gettysburg Visitors Center, Cyclorama Building (demolished in 2013).

Richard Neutra. The Kaufmann House, Palm Springs, California. The house was designed by Neutra in 1946. It was commissioned by Edgar J. Kaufmann, Sr., a Pittsburgh department store tycoon as a desert retreat from harsh winters.

Rudolph Michael Schindler was born into a
Jewish Viennese family in 1887. A contemporary
and life-long friend of Richard Neutra, he also
moved to Los Angeles via Chicago, where he
worked with Frank Lloyd Wright.

A radical modernist, his work was only later
admired for its inventiveness and character.

Today, three of his works, the Fitzpatrick-Leland
House, the Mackey Apartments and the Schindler
House (Residence) in Los Angeles belong to the
Austrian Museum of Applied Arts/ Contemporary
Art (MAK). They are used for exhibitions and
housing of artists in residence.

"As if there had never been houses before."

- Reyner Banham
English architecture critic

Rudolf Schindler. Schindler House, West Hollywood, California (1921-1922).

Rudolf Schindler. Fitzpatrick-Leland House, Los Angeles, California (1936).

Rudolf Schindler. Mackey Apartments, Los Angeles, California (1939).

SSISSIPPI

ALABAMA

MISSOURI

MICHIGAN

WE A
THAT BEFORE
TERRIBLE STRUGGLE
THROUGHOUT THE W
ON THE ONE HAN
FORC

Friedrich St. Florian Born in 1932 in Graz, Austria, Friedrich St. Florian first moved to the United States on a Fulbright Scholarship in 1961. He is best known as the architect of The National World War II Memorial in Washington, DC.

The World War II Memorial honors the 16 million who served in the armed forces of the U.S., the more than 400,000 who died, and all who supported the war effort from home. Symbolic of the defining event of the 20th Century, the memorial is a monument to the spirit, sacrifice, and commitment of the American people. The Second World War is the only 20th Century event commemorated on the National Mall's central axis.

ECONOMISTS & SCIENTISTS

Most of the second and third generation of the notable *Austrian School of Economics* started by Carl Menger – explaining economic behavior in terms of utility – emigrated to the United States, where today they are known as advocates of free markets, and opponents of state regulation under the label of *Austrian Economics*. Refugees Ludwig von Mises, Oskar Morgenstern, Fritz Machlup, and Gottfried von Haberler all received top-notch academic appointments at Ivy League schools and helped reshape American economic thinking. Friedrich von Hayek looked for better opportunities first in London and then at the University of Chicago – he earned a Nobel Prize. Harvard University offered a chair to the prolific Joseph Schumpeter, a former Austrian Finance Minister, in the early 1930s. Schumpeter became one of the best known economists of his generation.

Peter Drucker came to the United States via London and advanced to the status of America's premier *management guru*. Trained mathematician Paul Lazarsfeld first went to the U.S. on a Rockefeller fellowship in 1932. An avid Socialist youth leader in his native Vienna, he pioneered systematic sociological survey research in the U.S. and became a leader in studies of mass communication and factors in people's decision making in politics and retail. As professor of sociology at Columbia University he trained dozens of students in his sophisticated methodologies. Financed by the Ford Foundation, Lazarsfeld along with Oskar Morgenstern launched the "Institute of Advance Study" (*Institut für Höhere Studien*) in Vienna in 1963, which became the premier training ground for Austrian social scientists (Pelinka). In their academic positions, these Austrian émigrés, who had made Vienna a haven of innovation in the social sciences between the wars, contributed mightily to making American universities leading institutions of higher education in the world.

Most of the second and third generation of the notable *Austrian School of Economics* emigrated to the United States, where today they are known as advocates of free markets, and opponents of state regulation under the label of *Austrian Economics*.

Austrian scientists have flocked to the U.S. ever since the exodus of the Vienna Jews in 1938 – including Nobel Prize winner in physics Wolfgang Pauli, Victor Weisskopf, an atomic physicist who taught at Harvard University, and Nobel Prize winner in medicine Eric Kandel, a neuroscientist at Columbia University. More recently biotech researchers such as Norbert Bischofberger have made a name for themselves.

Carl Menger, economist and the founder of
the Austrian School of Economics

Ludwig von Mises, Austrian School economist, New York University.

Friedrich August von Hayek, photographed here in ca. 1930. Economist and philosopher, Nobel Prize in Economic Sciences, 1974.

Austrian scientists have flocked to the U.S. ever since the exodus of the Vienna Jews in 1938.

Wolfgang Pauli, Nobel Prize in Physics, 1945.

Peter Drucker, often described as the "founder of modern management."

Eric Kandel, Neuroscientist. Nobel Prize in Physiology or Medicine, 2000.

Victor Frederick Weisskopf, nuclear physicist, 1957. Weisskopf was Group Leader of the Theoretical Division of the *Manhattan Project* at Los Alamos. Later he spoke out against the proliferation of nuclear weapons.

Martin Karplus is a theoretical chemist and Professor Emeritus at Harvard University. He was awarded the Nobel Prize in Chemistry in 2013.

Nary an American ski resort exists that did not have Austrian involvement

SKI PIONEERS AND THE MAKING OF AMERICAN WINTER RESORTS

American railroad tycoon and banker Averell Harriman pioneered the first American winter resort in Sun Valley, Idaho. As chairman of the Union Pacific Railroad he got his company to invest 1,5 million into a new ski resort (lodge, chair lifts, ski runs) to transport more passengers on Union Pacific, the railroad he headed in the 1930s. The Austrian Count Felix Schaffgotsch had consulted with Harriman in finding the site for a new ski resort. Austrian ski instructors such as Friedl Pfeiffer from Hannes Schneider's famous ski school in St. Anton, Tyrol, helped make it into a new skiing Mecca in the American West, instructing many Hollywood celebrities in this attractive new sport. These good-looking *Naturburschen* (nature boys) from the Austrian Alps, most of them with only basic elementary school educations, started as ski instructors – many of them becoming entrepreneurs in the winter sports industry. With their heavy foreign accents they also brought yodeling and *Gemütlichkeit* to the Rockies and created the "alpine" flair that came to define skiing in the U.S. Ski champions like Pfeiffer also trained American Olympic skiing teams. Winter sports in the U.S., in fact, had been pioneered already before World War I in Lake Placid in upstate New York, as well as through Dartmouth College's pioneering collegiate ski competitions. In 1923 Anton Diettrich began coaching the Dartmouth ski team. In the early 1930s snow trains began transporting skiiers from Boston and New York to fledgling resort towns such as Franconia and North Conway, New Hampshire, and Stowe, Vermont, and from San Francisco up to the high Sierras. In the mid-1930s, winter sports shows in the Boston Garden and New York's Madison Square Garden featured Austrian skiing champions such a Hannes Schneider and Otto Lang promoting skiing in the United States.

In 1939 Hannes Schneider, now a refugee from Nazi Germany, began directing the ski school on Mount Cranmore in North Conway, New Hampshire. He brought the *Arlberg ski technique* to the U.S., which he helped pioneer in the 1930s in St. Anton. Schneider was also a pioneer in promoting skiing through films. He brought numerous instructors from his St. Anton ski school such as Lang and Pfeiffer and Luggi Főger (Badger Pass, California) to American resorts. Ski resorts began to spring up on the West Coast from Washington to California. Hans Schroll was a yodeling Austrian ski fanatic. With an investment from Walt Disney, whom he taught how to ski, Schroll launched the first California ski resort, *Sugar Bowl*, late in 1939. Another Austrian, Bill Klein was its first ski school director. Located near Donner Pass not far from Lake Tahoe, many resorts such as *Squaw Valley* (site of the 1960 Winter Olympics) and *Heavenly Valley* were to follow after World War II.

Ski area marketers defined Colorado after World War II as "home to the Alps, Victorian high society, and the Wild West" (Coleman). Friedl Pfeiffer pioneered Aspen as a ski resort. Pepi Gramshammer added Alpine authenticity to Vail with his Tyrolean-style lodge in the early 1960s. Billy Kidd, Olympic slalom silver medalist in the Innsbruck Olympics in 1964, promoted Steamboat Springs. They all fueled resort town images – Vail's alpine village, Aspen's Victorian cosmopolitanism, or Steamboat's American West. Josef "Pepi" Stiegler won the slalom gold medal in the Innsbruck Olympics in 1964. He moved to the U.S. in 1965 to become the director of ski school in Jackson Hole, Wyoming, where his brother also opened a Tyrolean restaurant. He stayed on as director for almost 30 years – two of his children also became champion skiers. Nary an American ski resort exists that did not have Austrian involvement.

Friedl Pfeiffer, Elli and Fred Iselin in Aspen, Colorado, 1954.

Hannes and Herbert Schneider with Edi Mall at Mount Cranmore, North Conway, New Hampshire, 1954.

Friedl Pfeiffer and Elli Iselin in Aspen, Colorado, 1954.

CHEFS AND AUSTRIAN CUISINE

Austria has a long and great tradition of vocational training in many fields such as woodworking, baking, and cooking. Such well-trained Austrian chefs have been successful with their restaurants and catering businesses in the United States. Like Austria's skiers, its chefs have come to the United States with little formal schooling but with much innate entrepreneurial talent. Wolfgang Puck, Kurt Gutenbrunner, and Thomas Ferlesch are prime examples of such successful chefs/entrepreneurs. Carinthian-born Wolfgang Puck learned cooking on his mother's side. He is probably best known for his restaurants and cooking shows, and his catering of the Academy Award ceremonies.

Lower Austrian-born Kurt Gutenbrunner and Vienna-born Thomas Ferlesch have been successful chefs and restaurateurs in New York City. Gutenbrunner grew up in the small village on the Danube Walsé, which also became the name of his first New York restaurant opened in 2000. He did his training in Vienna and Munich and learned about Austrian wine culture in the Wachau region outside of Vienna. In 2001 Ronald Lauder hired him to run *Café Sabarsky* in his lovely museum of Viennese art and design, *Neue Gallerie.* Over time, *Blaue Gans* and *The Upholstery Store* in the West Village were added to the growing Gutenbrunner restaurant empire. In his cookbook *Neue Cuisine* (2011) he featured more than 100 of his favorite recipes from *Wienerschnitzel* to *Apfelstrudel.*

Thomas Ferlesch learned about baking and organic food preparation from his family and later went to cooking school in Vienna. After 37 years of cooking in New York City with mentors such as George Lang at Café des Artistes, he opened his own restaurant *Werkstatt* (workshop) in Brooklyn, where he fuses his favorite New York dishes (soft shell crabs, shad, and roe) with traditional Austrian cuisine (*Sauerbraten* and *Gulyash*). French influences inform signature dishes such *Bourride with Aioli* ("a second cousin to bouillabaisse" with saffron), not to mention *Milchrahmstrudel* for desert.

Friedl Pfeiffer (1911-1995)

Friedl Pfeiffer was an Austrian ski instructor from Hannes Schneider's famous ski school in St. Anton, Tyrol and a winter sport entrepreneur in Aspen, Colorado. Pfeiffer first came to the U.S. (via Australia) in 1938 to work as a ski instructor in America's first winter resort, Sun Valley, stamped out of the ground in 1937 by Averell Harriman and the Union Pacific Railroad. Pfeiffer also made a name for himself in ski racing. In 1939 he took over the *Sun Valley* ski school and helped making it into a new skiing Mecca in the American West, instructing many Hollywood celebrities in this attractive new sport. Pfeiffer also trained American Olympic skiing teams. He married a wealthy banker's daughter from Salt Lake City, Utah. When the U.S. entered World War II, *enemy aliens* like Pfeiffer were arrested as potential Nazi spies. He volunteered for the 10TH Mountain Division in the U.S. Army. While training in Camp Hale, CO, he first saw the beautiful Aspen Valley. Pfeiffer fought in Italy and was wounded badly in April 1945. He returned to the U.S. and became a founder of the Aspen, Colorado, winter resort – The Aspen Ski Corporation, the Aspen Ski School, and Buttermilk Mountain after the war. He brought ski racing to Aspen (the 1950 World Championships) and initiated popular parallel slalom professional competitions. He is an inductee of the 1987 Aspen Hall of Fame (Bischof; Traussnig, 151-206).

Wolfgang Puck (1949-)

Wolfgang Puck was born in Carinthia and learned cooking by his mother's side (Puck). He is probably best known for his restaurants and cooking shows, his catering of the Academy Award ceremonies, and brash marketeering of his cookware on television. After his apprenticeship in Austria and training with French chefs he moved to the U.S. in 1973 and to Los Angeles in 1975. In 1981 he published his first cook book *Modern French Cuisine for the American Kitchen* and opened his *Spago* restaurant (the 1994 *James Beard Restaurant of the Year*), where House Smoked Salmon Pizza became his signature dish (his pizzas originated from his cooking experience in *Provence*, not from Italy). With his enormous success as a "foodie entrepreneur," he launched a number of companies expanding his restaurant empire (now also including *Wolfgang Puck Express* shops in numerous airports around the world), moving into catering services and licensed products (like pressure cookers). In 2017 he received a star on the Hollywood Walk of Fame for his work on television and in film. He also has built a sterling reputation as a serious philanthropist, raising money for *Meals on Wheels* and cancer research.

Norbert Bischofberger (1955-)

Norbert Bischofberger is a biochemist from Mellau, a small village in Vorarlberg, and one of the inventors of the antiviral drug *Tamiflu*, generically known as *Oseltamivir*, as well as antiviral drugs against Aids and Hepatitis B. Tamiflu is the only oral medication on the market to treat influenza A and B as well as the 2009 Pandemic H1N1 (*swine flu*), the spread of which caused an ongoing pandemic in 2009. Bischofberger served as the Executive Vice President, Research and Development and Chief Scientific Officer at *Gilead Sciences*, a biopharmaceutical company in Foster City, CA, specializing in antivirals for almost thirty years. Bischofberger earned his Bachelor of Science degree in Chemistry from the University of Innsbruck, and his PhD in Organic Chemistry from the Swiss Institute of Technology (ETH Zurich). He did his postdoctoral work at Harvard University and with *Syntex Research*. In terms of the risk viruses pose for mankind he is pessimistic, saying, "I think the threat by new bacterial or viral agents is higher than the potential of a nuclear war." He recently left Gilead to launch the new start-up *Kronos Bio* with MIT professor Angela Koehler. They are taking a shot at breaking new ground in cancer R&D.

For more information

and multimedia content,
visit the book's companion site at

www.austriainusa.org

Chapter 6

Austrian - American Relations: Political, Economic, Cultural, 1955 to the Present

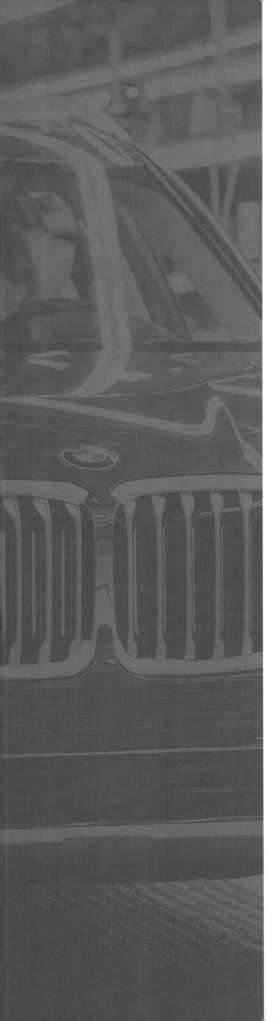

The signing of the Austrian State Treaty ended the ten-year four-power occupation of the country – permanently neutral Austria graduated to become an important Cold War mediator. Austria's active neutrality policy made it a Cold War troubleshooter during times of high tension. Official relations with the U.S. were solid, in spite of protests against the Vietnam War in the 1960s. During the crises in the Communist Bloc in Hungary (1956), Czechoslovakia (1968), and Poland (1981), Austria welcomed hundreds of thousands of refugees. In the 1980s President Ronald Reagan castigated Austrians for their active trade relations with the Communist Bloc. Officials in Reagan's Justice Department also put Kurt Waldheim, democratically elected as President in 1986, on the "watch list" of persons not welcomed to the United States, due to his controversial role as an officer in the Balkans during World War II. With the Cold War ending in 1989, Austria moved "westward" and joined the European Union in 1995 but did not become a member of NATO like many neighbors to the East. Austrians were shocked about the 9/11 terrorist attacks. However, Austria did not join the "coalition of the willing" in President George W. Bush's invasion of Iraq in 2003 for lack of a mandate by the UN Security Council. President Bush visited Austria for a day in 2006. Austrians were enamored with President Obama and have been critical of President Trump.

AUSTRIANS AS COLD WAR MEDIATORS

The Soviet condition for Austria to finally get a State Treaty in 1955 was to neutralize the country – the U.S. was not so happy with this outcome but the Eisenhower Administration accepted it as a price to pay to finally evacuate the country from its postwar four-power occupation. In the following years, Austria needed to define its role as a permanently neutral country on the East-West fault line of the Cold War (Bischof/Kofler). The government of Julius Raab developed an armed and active neutrality policy like Switzerland.

The Soviet condition for Austria to finally get a State Treaty in 1955 was to neutralize the country – the U.S. was not so happy with this outcome but the Eisenhower Administration accepted it as a price to pay to finally evacuate the country from its postwar four-power occupation.

Nikita Khrushchev shakes Jackie Kennedy's hand during the Vienna Summit 1961.

Jimmy Carter and Leonid Brezhnev share a kiss on the cheek during the SALT II talks in Vienna, 1975.

The first big test came during the Hungarian Revolution in the fall of 1956, when the new Austrian *Bundesheer* was staged on the border and some 180,000 Hungarian refugees fled to Austria. Most went on to live in the U.S. and other Western countries (Graf/Knoll). Raab's Foreign Minister (1959-66) Bruno Kreisky practiced Austrian *"Ostpolitik" avant la lettre*, trying to mediate between chairman Nikita Khrushchev and his old friend Willi Brand in the Berlin crisis (Rathkolb). In early June 1961 President John F. Kennedy met Khrushchev for a summit meeting in Vienna, again discussing the Berlin issue as the principal bone of contention at the time, next to a series of crisis points in the Global South from Laos to Congo to Cuba. Talks in Vienna left the Berlin issue unresolved. Despite Kreisky's and Kennedy's mediation efforts, only two months after the Vienna summit the Berlin Wall was built to stop the flow of refugees to the West (Bischof et al., Vienna Summit).

Austria played a particularly active role in East-West mediation during the détente phase of the Cold War in the 1970s (Gilde). U.S. Ambassador Henry Grunwald has called Vienna "an unofficial headquarters for the Cold War" (Grunwald, 597). During the crisis in Czechoslovakia after the invasion of the Warsaw Pact troops, Austria again served as a haven for refugees. Both Presidents Nixon and Ford stopped over in Salzburg in 1972/75 on trips dealing with the Middle East. Chancellor Kreisky briefed Nixon and Kissinger on their way to a tour of the Near East in early June 1972. In early June 1975 President Gerald Ford met Egyptian President Anwar Sadat for a meeting on Near Eastern issues. During his opening press conference Ford noted: "Your hospitality in offering Salzburg as the site for my meetings with President Sadat reflects Austria's constructive international policy and the traditional warmth of the Austrian nation." At the same time Austrian diplomats played a crucial role in negotiating human rights issues in the preparatory sessions for the Helsinki Conference of Security and Cooperation in Europe in 1975, markedly reducing Cold War tensions. In May 1979

President Jimmy Carter met Soviet Party Chief Leonid Brezhnev in a Vienna summit to sign the SALT II treaty. After the Soviet invasion of Afghanistan half a year later, Cold War tensions resumed again and the US Senate never ratified the SALT II treaty. Austria punched above her weight in the United Nations, particularly with its three stints as a non-permanent member of the Security Council in 1973/74, 1991/92, and 2009/10.

AUSTRIA AND THE U.S.: FROM COLD WAR TO POST-COLD WAR

During the Cold War Austria was the superpowers' "darling" of sorts. As a Cold War neutral it played a "special role" between East and West, especially as a "mediator" and "bridge builder." Vienna hosted two summits in 1961 and 1979 as well as long-running arms control talks (Conventional Force Reduction Talks). As a U.N. Headquarter, Vienna has also been hosting Vienna also has been hosting the U.N.'s "International Atomic Energy Agency" (IAEA). Austria played a crucial role in the CSCE negotiations in the group of Neutral & Non-Aligned States and after the Cold War came to host the CSCE Headquarters in Vienna. Vienna also hosted the Organization of Petroleum Exporting Countries (OPEC) during and after the Cold War. The U.S. respected Austrian neutrality, especially Kreisky's "active neutrality" policy. Austria also continued to profit handsomely from the Marshall Plan's counterpart funds through the "ERP-Fund" established in 1962. The U.S. tolerated Austria's growing trade with Eastern Europe's Soviet satellite; only in the 1980s did President Ronald Reagan criticize Austrian "high tech" exports to the Soviet Bloc. Austria continued its stance as a "secret ally" of the West, even though its neutrality did not permit joining NATO and the trans-Atlantic structures. Given its strong trading relationship with West Germany, Moscow prohibited Austria from joining the European Economic Community, fearing a renewed *Anschluss*.

Austrian-American relations experienced strains due to the election of Kurt Waldheim in 1986. Waldheim served as the two-time Secretary General of the United Nations in New York (1972-1981). However, when Waldheim's controversial World War II past came to light during the election campaign, the U.S. Justice Department "blacklisted" him by putting him on their "watch list" of undesirable aliens not welcomed to the U.S. Even though Waldheim's involvement in Nazi war crimes in the Balkans theater of war could never be proven, the U.S. refused to remove him off the "watch list" after his election to serve as Austria's President (1986-1992). Reagan's Ambassador Henry Grunwald was supposed to "take the strain out of the atmosphere between Washington and Vienna" (Grunwald, 622). Grunwald was surprised to be asked by James Baker, George Bush's Secretary of State who met the Russian Foreign Minister Eduard Shevardnaze in Vienna in 1989, whether Austrians spoke German "or some other language" (Grunwald, 618). Such basic ignorance sometimes made improving bilateral relations more difficult.

The end of the Cold War, which began to happen on the Austrian-Hungarian border in the first half of 1989, dramatically changed Austria's international status. In June 1989, Austria's and Hungary's Foreign Ministers Alois Mock and Gyula Horn, cut the iron curtain and provided the iconic picture for the ending of the Cold War in Central Europe. When the iron curtain came down along the Austrian-Hungarian border. This inspired East Germans on holidays in Hungary in the summer of 1989 to cross the border into Austria and then go to West Germany. This East German exodus contributed to the destabilization of the East German regime in the fall of 1989 and led to East Germans ignoring the Berlin Wall later in the year. These events contributed mightily to ending the Cold War. In 1989 Austria applied to join the European Economic Community and finally became a member of the European Union in 1995. Austrian foreign

policy became part and parcel of EU-foreign relations. Austria thus moved more to the West but did not join NATO as most of Moscow's former satellites in Eastern Europe did. The repercussions of the civil wars and break-up of Yugoslavia in the 1990s affected Austria intimately. Along with Germany, Austria recognized the new states of Slovenia and Croatia early on. Austria received tens of thousands of refugees from the Western Balkans region (esp. from Bosnia) and Austrian civil society donated generously in aid to the peoples affected by these civil wars. Austrian diplomats such as Wolfgang Petritsch and former Chancellor Franz Vranitzky and Vice Chancellor Erhard Busek played crucial roles as mediators in these conflicts sparked by the break-up of Yugoslavia in the 1990s (Petritsch). During Austria's first EU Presidency in 1998, Austria pushed hard for the accession to the EU of her neighbors – the former Soviet satellites.

In the immediate post-Cold War era, the U.S. emerged as a hegemonic "hyper power" and Austrians accepted their new "dwarf" status in the EU. Austria's politicians and the public were shocked about the 9/11 attacks on New York and Washington and professed their deep sympathy to the victims and the American public. The Austrian state television channel ORF reported from New York and Washington for forty-three hours straight – longer than German TV. The initial reaction among Austrians quickly morphed into a discourse about their neutrality. In a highly partisan debate many Austrians felt "lucky" to be neutral, as their benign neutral status allowed the country to stay out of the looming conflict. While the government supported American retaliation against Afghanistan, the Austrian public at large did not. Austrians were even more critical about Bush's war against Iraq. Austria was part of "old Europe" and did not join Bush's "coalition of the willing" to fight in Iraq – Austria also adhered to strict neutrality and prohibited American and NATO use of its airspace during the Iraq crisis (Reiter in: Reiter/Embacher, 161-192, here 177, 188). Public opinion slipped into dumb

Vienna Summit, 1961 John F. Kennedy (left) sits next to Adolf Schärf and Nikita Khrushchev on a bench in Vienna's Hofburg Palace.

President Richard Nixon (left) arrives in Salzburg on June 10, 1974 and is greeted by Federal Chancellor Bruno Kreisky (standing next to him) and Foreign Minister Rudolf Kirchschläger (standing behind Nixon).

anti-Americanism and *Schadenfreude*. While anti-Americanism on the left fell back on its old patterns of blaming 'U.S. imperialism,' the right, which had never forgiven the Americans for defeating Hitler, blamed American "hubris, money and power" for having caused the 9/11 attacks. As historian Brandon Keene puts it: "there exists in Austrian culture an underlying resentment for dominant political power in other parts of the world, coupled with their realization that Austria never has regained the power position it had in the world before World War I." He adds, that Austrian public opinion turned anti-American quickly in 2003, like in the Austrian reaction to the U.S.'s "blacklisting" of Waldheim with the "watch-list" decision: "Austrians are prone to forming drastic opinions of the United States, and rather fast" (Keene, 1).

During Austria's second EU-Presidency in the first half of 2006, President Bush spent a one-day visit in Vienna for a summit with EU leaders. During the Cold War American presidents visited Vienna a number of times; this happened rarely in the post-Cold War era. Austrians were thrilled over the election of Barack Obama in 2008. Many of the important Cold War Atlantic institutions like NATO, set into place by President Truman's liberal world order regime in the early Cold War, can no longer be taken for granted during the Presidency of Donald Trump.

The third Austrian EU-Presidency in the second half of 2018, coinciding with the 180th anniversary of the diplomatic relations between Austria and the U.S., saw a flurry of Austrian Ministerial visits to DC (Ministers of the Economy, Interior, Justice, Higher Education, as well as the Speaker of the Austrian Parliament). Shortly after, in mid-February 2019, the Austrian Federal Chancellor Sebastian Kurz was received at the White House by President Donald Trump for an extended bilateral meeting followed by a delegation meeting including the highest office holders of the U.S. Administration.

OPEC headquarters in Vienna.

AUSTRIAN BUSINESS IN THE UNITED STATES

Austrian companies and their U.S. branches currently provide work for some 40,000 people in the United States, predominantly in the manufacturing sector (Austrian National Bank). In addition, the United States today are the second most important destination for Austrian exports and rank fourth for Austrian foreign direct investment (FDI).

Trade volumes (both exports and imports) have been growing steadily over the past years. Whereas in 1985 Americans exported $441 million of goods to Austria, they imported $833 million. In 2017 Americans exported $4,264 million worth of goods to Austria, while importing a whopping $11,721 million from Austria. Although 70 percent of Austrian exports go to European Union member states, the U.S. at the time of this publication are Austria's fourth largest trading partner after Germany, Switzerland and Italy, and its second-largest export market after Germany. The U.S. exports to Austria are mainly chemicals and pharmaceuticals, machines and motor vehicles, and manufactured goods.

What are Austrian businesses operating in the United States? In 2016, the Austrian steel giant *VOEST* finished a new production facility in Corpus Christi, Texas for a basis investment of USD 740 million – to date the largest investment ever made by an Austrian company in the United States. It is the world's largest and most advanced plant of its type and produces around two tons of high-quality *Hot Briquette Iron*, a pre-material in steel production, each year. *Schoeller Bleckmann Oilfield Equipment* produces drilling pipes for U.S. companies. *Steyr Works* export Diesel engines to the U.S. for BMW X-Series SUVs built in South Carolina. Americans import KTM motorcycles from Austria, while Austrians buy Harley Davidsons. The Salzburg crane builder *Palfinger* contributed most

to crane sales to the United States. The Carinthian arms manufacturer *Glock* exports guns and ammunition to the United States. A world leader in semi-automatic pistols, Glock is the weapon of choice in many U.S. law enforcement agencies today. In addition, Austria also sells aircraft and aircraft components to the United States. On the culinary side, Austrian wines (especially *Grüner Veltliner* grape) have become increasingly popular with American fine diners. Americans love the energy drink *Red Bull*, which dominates the industry.

Austrian businesses like *Palfinger* and *Rosenbauer*, *Alpla* and *Grass*, are flying under the radar and have built substantial market shares in the United States. Alpla is a family business with 176 locations in 45 countries (including a dozen plants in the U.S. with headquarters in Atlanta). They are leaders in the market for packaging systems, particularly plastic containers. Grass produces movement systems for the kitchen and bath, with office facilities around the U.S. Grass is also known for its workforce training. Rosenbauer is a specialist in the production of fire trucks and fire equipment. Rosenbauer Minnesota, one of Rosenbauer America's four production sites, is located in Wyoming, MN. The plant specializes in custom vehicles, technically demanding fire service trucks, which are manufactured according to individual customer requirements. Salzburg based crane manufacturer Palfinger is now one of the leading truck equipment manufacturers offering a comprehensive product portfolio of cranes, hooklifts, cable hoists, forklifts, liftgates, service bodies, and platforms. With a number of production facilities in Canada and the U.S., Palfinger employs more than 1,000 people in North America. Palfinger holds the top position in market share in many of its business units. Austrian businesses also have a strong record in "green technologies" with a focus on sustainability.

A KTM RC 390 motorbike. KTM bikes have been winning the *Dakar Rally* for sixteen years straight.

Palfinger founded in 1932 has been producing lifting solutions for use on commercial vehicles and in the maritime field.

Austrian companies and their U.S. branches currently provide work for some 40,000 people in the United States, predominantly in the manufacturing sector (Austrian National Bank). In addition, the United States today are the second most important destination for Austrian exports and rank fourth for Austrian foreign direct investment (FDI).

Trade volumes (both exports and imports) have been growing steadily over the past years.

Alpla's North America headquarters in McDonough, Georgia. The international plastics processor, another *hidden champion* from Austria, has been active in the United States since 2001.

Austrian steelmaker *voestalpine Group* has been investing heavily in the United States.

Engines made in Austria go into many BMW products manufactured in the United States. Overall, more than one out of two newly-sold BMW and MINI vehicles delivered worldwide are powered by an engine from *Steyr*.

Shown here is the 4.5 millionth BMW built in the U.S. rolling off the assembly line at BMW Group Plant Spartanburg in South Carolina. September 8, 2019 marks 25 years of BMW production in the United States.

Henry A. Grunwald
(1922-2005)

Born Heinz Anatol Grünwald in Vienna, he was the son of famous librettist Alfred Grünwald, who wrote libretti for operettas by Lehár, Kálmán, and Oscar Straus. After the 1938 *Anschluss*, the Grunwald family managed to escape "Nazi Austria" via Czechoslovakia, Paris, Biarritz, Casablanca, and Lisbon, arriving in New York City in 1940. After studying philosophy at New York University, he worked his way up in *TIME* Magazine from copy boy to editor in chief. After serving 11 years as *Time's* managing editor, Grunwald took on the role of editor-in-chief of all of Time, Inc.'s magazines, including *Fortune, Sports Illustrated, People* and *Money*, and running the Time empire until 1987 when President Ronald Reagan appointed him U.S. Ambassador to his native Austria, a post he held until 1990. Grunwald's memoirs *One Man's America* (1997) provide a lot of information about the difficult process of assimilation for refugees but are a love song to his adopted home America. He observed: "every immigrant is a permanent student of his substitute home, of its customs and rules, its public as well as its secret dreams" (Grunwald, 43). So for example, while young Henry launched a successful career as a journalist, his famous librettist father could never adapt to his new "cultural habitat" with its different "audience tastes and theatrical fashions" (Grunwald, 45).

Max Hollein (1969 -)

Born in Vienna in 1969, Hollein studied art history at the University of Vienna and business administration at the Vienna University of Economics. He moved to New York City to take on the position of project director of exhibitions at the Solomon R. Guggenheim Museum in New York. He also worked closely with Guggenheim's director, as "Chief of Staff and Manager of European Relations," responsible for key projects such as the establishment of the exhibition halls Guggenheim Berlin and Guggenheim Las Vegas, and the Guggenheim Bilbao. He then served as Director of Schirn Kunsthalle, Städel Museum, and Liebieghaus Skulpturensammlung in Frankfurt/Germany. He returned to the U.S. in 2016 to serve as Director and CEO of the Fine Arts Museums of San Francisco, overseeing the de Young and the Legion of Honors museums. In April 2018, the Metropolitan Museum of Art announced that Hollein would become its 10th director. Hollein has been reflecting "on the role of encyclopedic art museums in our time and what I see as a breathtaking combination of opportunity and responsibility." Since the Met's founding 150 years ago, the role of the encyclopedic museum has been changing from an effort to bring all the cultures of the world together in one place to "stories" being told in our "globalized, interconnected world" (Hollein).

In *Vogue* magazine's estimation: "Hollein, who as of this August is the Met's tenth director, strikes many people as being preposterously well qualified for the position. Forty-nine years old and armed with degrees in art history and business administration, he has already directed five museums and overseen the fund-raising and building of a new wing for one of them. He's curated shows that range from old-master art to Pablo Picasso and Jeff Koons, and delivered excellent admissions. He gets along equally well with artists, curators, board members, donors, and scholars. The only downside to his appointment is that he's not a woman" (Kazanjian).

Bibliography

Select Bibliography

General

Bischof Günter. *Relationships/Beziehungsgeschichten: Austria and the United States in the Twentieth Century* (TRANSATLANTICA 4). Innsbruck: StudienVerlag 2014

Daniels Roger. *Coming to America: A History of Immigration and Ethnicity in American Life.* 2nd ed. New York: Perennial 2002

Drimmel Heinrich. *Die Antipoden: Die Neue Welt in den USA und das Österreich vor 1918.* Vienna: Amalthea, 1984

Easterlin Richard A./David Ward/William S. Bernard/Reed Ueda. *Immigration.* Cambridge, MA: Harvard UP 1982

Hölbling Walter/Reinhold Wagnleitner, eds. *The European Emigrant Experience in the U.S.A.* Tübingen: Gunter Narr 1992

Horvath Traude/Gerda Neyer, eds. *Auswanderungen aus Österreich: von der Mitte des 19. Jahrhunderts bis zur Gegenwart.* Vienna: Böhlau 1996

Luebke Frederick C. "Austrians." In: Stephan Thernstrom, ed. *Harvard Encyclopedia of American Ethnis Groups.* Cambridge, MA: Harvard University Press 1980, 164-71

Matsch Erwin. Wien – *Washington: Ein Journal diplomatischer Beziehungen* 1838-1917, Vienna: Böhlau 1990

Reimers David M. *Still the Golden Door: The Third World Comes to America.* New York: Columbia UP 1985

Spaulding E. Wilder. *Quiet Invaders: The Story of the Austrian Impact upon America.* Vienna: Bundesverlag 1968

U.S. Embassy Vienna, ed. *175 Years: U.S.- Austrian Diplomatic Relations. Vienna 2013*

Towards The American Century

CHAPTER 1

Albrich Thomas. *Goldjäger aus Tirol: "Von Kitzbühel nach Kalifornien über Kufstein"; Das Tagebuch des Joseph Steinberger 1851/52.* Innsbruck: StudienVerlag, 2008.

Auman Karen. "'English Liberties' and German Settlers in Colonial America: The Georgia Salzburgers' Conceptions of Community, 1730-1750." *Early American Studies: An Interdisciplinary Journal,* vol. 11, no. 1 (Winter 2013): 37-54

Herz Dietmar and John David Smith. "Into Danger but also Closer to God": The Salzburgers' Voyage to Georgia, 1733-1734. *The Georgia Historical Quarterly,* vol. 80, no. 1 (Spring 1996): 1-26

Hofer J. M. "Georgia Salzburgers." *The Georgia Historical Quarterly,* vol. 18, no. 2 (June 1934): 99-117

Milton Rubincam. "Historical Background of the Salzburger Emigration to Georgia." *The Georgia Historical Quarterly,* vol. 35, no. 2 (June, 1951): 99-115

Matsch Erwin. *Wien – Washington: Ein Journal diplomatischer Beziehungen 1838-1917,* Vienna: Böhlau 1990

James Van Horn Melton. "Alpine Miner to Low-Country Yeoman: The Transatlantic Worlds of a Georgia Salzburger 1693-1761." *Past & Present,* no. 201 (Nov., 2008): 97-140

------. *Religion, Community, and Slavery on the Colonial Southern Frontier.* New York: Cambridge University Press 2015

Phelps Nicole M.. *U.S.-Habsburg Relations from 1815 to the Paris Peace Conference: Sovereignty Transformed.* Cambridge: Cambridge University Press 2013

Salzburger Landesregierung, ed., *Reformation – Emigration: Protestanten in Salzburg.* Ausstellung 21. Mai – 26. Oktober 1981 Schloss Goldegg – Pongau Land Salzburg. Salzburg 1981

Singerton Jonathan. *Empires on the Edge: The Habsburg Monarchy and the American Revolution, 1763-1789.* PhD diss., University of Edinburgh 2018

----------. "'Some of Distinction Here Are Warm for the Part of America': Knowledge of and Sympathy for the American Cause in the Habsburg Monarchy, 1763-1783." *Journal of Austrian-American History,* vol 1, no 2 (2017): 128-158

----------. "Beginning Her World Anew: Maria von Born" https://jonathansingerton.com/2017/07/20/beginning-her-world-anew-maria-von-born/

Schmidl Erwin A. "Austrians in Mexico, 1864-1867." In: Klaus Eisetere/Günter Bischof, eds., *Transatlantic Relations: Austria and Latin America in the 19th an 20th Centuries* (TRANSATLANTICA 2). Innsbruck: StudienVerlag 2006, 49-56

Steidl Annemarie /Wladimir Fischer-Nebmaier/James W. Oberly. *From a Multiethnic Empire to a Nation of Nations: Austro Hungarian Migrants in the US,* 1870–1940 (TRANSATLANTICA vol. 10). Innsbruck: StudienVerlag, 2016

CHAPTER 2

"Austria on Display at the Chicago World's Columbian Exposition, 1893: A Collection of Sources." *Journal of Austrian-American History,* vol. 1, No. 2 (2017: 117-127

Bischof Günter. "Two Sides of the Coin: The Americanization of Austria and Austrian Anti-Americanism." I*n: idem. Relationships/Beziehungsgeschichten: Austria and the United States in the Twentieth Century* (TRANSATLANTICA 4). Innsbruck: StudienVerlag 2014, 25-56

McClain Aurora Wilson. "Meeting in St. Louis: American Encounters with Nascent European Modernism at the 1904 Louisiana Purchase Exposition." M.A. thesis, University of Texas-Austin 2015

McDowell Scott. "The Price of Sovereignty: Indemnification and the Lattimer Massacre of 1897," in: Marija Wakounig/Ferdinand Kühnel, eds., *Europa Orientalis* 20. Vienna/Berlin: Lit Verlag [forthcoming 2018]

Higham John. *Strangers in the Land: Patterns of American Nativism 1860-1925.* 16th ed. New York: Atheneum 1973 [1955]

Hoelbing Walter/Reinhold Wagnleitner, eds. T*he European Emigrant Experience in the U.S.A.* Tübingen: Gunther Narr 1992

Hoerder Dirk. "Migrations and Belonging." In Emily S. Rosenberg, ed., *A World Connecting 1870-1945* (Akira Iriye/Jürgen Osterhammel, eds. A History of the World). Cambridge, MA: Harvard UP 2012, 435-589.

K.K. Central-Comission für die Weltausstellung in Chicago 1893, ed. *Amtlicher Special-Katalog der Österreichischen Abtheilung auf der Weltausstellung in Chcago 1893.* Vienna: Johann N Vernay 1893

Kuzmany Börries, "Jüdische Programflüchtlinge in Österreich 1881/82 und die Professionialisierung der International Hilfe." In: Börries Kuzmany/Rita Gasternauer, eds. *Aufnahmeland Österreich: Über den Umgang mit Massflucht seit dem 18. Jahrhundert.* Vienna: Mandelbau 2017, 94-125

Larson Erik. *The Devil in the White City.* New York: Vintage 2003

Matsch Erwin. *Wien – Washington: Ein Journal diplomatischer Beziehungen 1838-1917,* Vienna: Böhlau 1990

Pichler Meinrad. *Auswanderer: Von Vorarlberg in die USA 1800-1938.* Bregenz: Vorarlberger Autoren Gesellschaft, 1993

Pollack Martin. *Kaiser von Amerika: Die grosse Flucht aus Galizien.* Vienna: Paul Zsolnay 2010

Steidl Annemarie /Wladimir Fischer-Nebmaier/James W. Oberly. *From a Multiethnic Empire to a Nation of Nations: Austro Hungarian Migrants in the US, 1870–1940* (TRANSATLANTICA vol. 10). Innsbruck: StudienVerlag 2016

------. "Migration Patterns in the Late Habsburg Empire," in: Günter Bischof/Dirk Rupnow, eds. *Migration in Austria* (CAS 26). New Orleans-Innsbruck: UNO-innsbruck university press 2017, 69-86

------. "Border Control in Ellis Island: Austro-Hungarians Crossing the Atlantic in the Age of Mass Migration" [2018 unpublished manuscript]

Zahra Tara. *The Great Departure: Mass Migration from Eastern Europe and the Making of the Free World.* New York: W.W. Norton 2016

CHAPTER 3

Adlgasser Franz. "The Roots of Communist Containment: American Food Aid in Austria and Hungary after World War I." in: Günter Bischof/Anton Pelinka/Rolf Steininger, eds., *Austria in the Nineteen Fifties* (CAS 3). New Brunswick, NJ: Transaction 1995, 171-188

Bednar Kurt. *Der Papierkrieg zwischen Washington und Wien* 1917/18. Innsbruck: StudienVerlag 2017

Berteau John S.. "U.S.-Austrian Relations in the Pre-Anschluss Period: FDR's Unwillingness for War," MA thesis, University of New Orleans 2007

Bischof Günter. "Austria's Loss – America's Gain: *finis Austria*—The "Anschluss" and the Expulsion Migration of Jewish Austrians to the U.S.," in: idem, *Relationships/Beziehungsgeschichten*, 57-82

------. "Busy with Refugee Work". Joseph Buttinger, Muriel Gardiner, and the Saving of Austrian Refugees, 1940–1941, in: Claudia Kuretsidis-Haider and Christine Schindler, eds. *Zeithistoriker – Archivar – Aufklärer: Festschrift für Winfried R. Garscha.* Vienna: DÖW 2017, 115-126

Coser Lewis A. *Refugee Scholars in America: Their Impact and Their Experiences.* New Haven: Yale UP 1984

Eppel Peter, ed., *Österreicher im Exil, USA 1938-1945: Eine Dokumentation* (Dokumentationsarchiv des Österreichischen Widerstandes) 2 vols. Vienna: Bundesverlag 1995

Fleck Christian. *Etablierung in der Fremde: Vertriebene Wissenschaftler in den USA nach 1933.* Frankfurt: Campus Verlag, 2015

Flügge Manfred. *Stadt Ohne Seele: Wien* 1938. Berlin: Aufbau 2018

Grunwald Henry. *One Man's America: A Journalist's Search for the Heart of His Country.* New York: Doubleday 1997

Heilbut Anthony. *Exiled in Paradise: German Refugee Artist and Intellectuals in America from 1930s to the Present.* Boston: Beacon Press 1983

Keyserlingk Robert H. *Austria in World War II: An Anglo-American Dilemma.* Kingston: McGill-Queen's University Press 1988

Klüger Ruth. *Weiter Leben. Eine Jugend.* Göttingen: Wallstein, 1992

Lackner Herbert. *Die Flucht der Dichter und Denker: Wie Europas Künstler und Wissenshcaftler den Nazis entkamen.* Vienna: Ueberreuther 2017

Lackner Robert. *Hugo Botstiber und das Wiener Konzerthaus: Leben und Wirken eines Kulturmanagers vom Fin De Si cle bis zum Anschluss.* Vienna: Böhlau 2016

Morton Frederic. *Runaway Waltz. A Memoir from Vienna to New York.* New York: Simon & Schuster, 2005

Pelinka Anton, "The Impact of American Scholarship on Austrian Political Science: The Making of a Discipline," in Günter Bischof/Anton Pelinka, eds *The Americanization/Westernization of Austria* (CAS 12). New Brunswick, NJ: Transaction, 2012, 226-34

Phelps Nicole M. *U.S.-Habsburg Relations from 1815 to the Paris Peace Conference.* Cambridge: Cambridge UP 2013

Strobl Philipp. "'Too Little to Live and Too Much to Die': The Burgenländers' Immigration to the United States During the Interwar Period." MA thesis, University of New Orleans 2009

-----. "Thinking Cosmopolitan or How Joseph became Joe Buttinger," in: Günter Bischof/Fritz Plasser/Eva Maltschnigg, eds. *Austrian Lives* (CAS 21). New Orleans – Innsbruck: UNO Press-innsbruck university press 2012, 92-122

------. "*…um der Notlage dieser Tage zu entfliehen": Die burgenländische Amerikawanderung der Zwischenkriegszeit.* Innsbruck: Studia 2015

Traussnig Florian. *Militärischer Widerstand von Aussen: Österreicher in der US-Armee und Kriegsgeheimdienst im Zweiten Weltkrieg.* Vienna: Böhlau 2015.

CHAPTER 4

Austrian Information (various issues)

Botstiber Dietrich W. *Not on the Mayflower.* Philadelphia 2007

Towards The American Century

Center Austria. *Center Austria: The Austrian Marshall Plan Center for European Studies/The University of New Orleans – 20 Years*. New Orleans: Self Published 2017

Bischof Günter/ Hans Petschar. *The Marshall Plan since 1947: Saving Europe, Rebuilding Austria*. Vienna: Brandstätter 2017

-------. *Relationships/Beziehungsgeschichten: Austria and the United States in the Twentieth Century*. Innsbruck: StudienVerlag 2014 (with Robert Lackner on Botstiber and Eva Maltschnig on GI brides), 183-96, 287-95

-------. *Austria in the First Cold War, 1945-1955: The Leverage of the Weak*. Basingstoke-New York: Macmillan-St. Martin's 1999

König Thomas. *Die Frühgeschichte des Fulbright Program in Österreich: Transatlantische "Fühlungsnahme auf dem Gebiet der Erziehung"*. Innsbruck: StudienVerlag 2012

Fulbright at Fifty: Austrian-American Educational Exchange 1950-2000. Vienna: Fulbright 2000

Komarnicka Olena. "Zwischen Erinnern und Vergessen: The Austrian Forum in New York und sein Beitrag zur Förderung des kollektiven Gedächtnisses," in: Evelyn Adunka/Primavera Driessen Gruber/Simon Usaty, eds., *Exilforschung: Österreich. Leistungen, Defizite & Perspektiven* (Exilforschung heute 4). Vienna: Mandelbaum 2018

Maltschnig Eva. "Austrian War Brides as Symbolic Border Guards," in: Marija Wakounig/Markus Peter Beham, eds., *Transgressing Boundaries: Humanities in Flux*, Vienna: Lit Verlag 2013, 229-44.

"Not on the Mayflower: Dietrich W. Botstiber's Journey from Anschluss Vienna to Philadelphia, 1938." *Journal of Austrian-American History* 1/1 (2017): 1-39

Rathkolb Oliver. *Washington ruft Wien: US-Grossmachtpolitik und Österreich 1953-1963*. Vienna: Böhlau 1997

Seidl Walter. *Zwischen Kultur und Culture: Das Austrian Institute in New York und Österreichs kulturelle Repräsentanz in den USA*. Vienna: Böhlau 2001

Wagnleitner Reinhold. *Coca-Colonization and the Cold War: The Cultural Mission of the United States in Austria after the Second World War,* transl. Diana Wolf. Chapel Hill: The University of North Carolina Press 1994

Witnah R. Donald/ Florentine E. Witnah. *Salzburg under Siege: U.S. Occupation, 1945-1955*. Westport, CT: Greenwood Press 1991

CHAPTER 5

Austrian Information 69 (Fall 2016): 18-29 (Hannes Richter on Gruen, Julian Steiner on Neutra, and Christoph Thun-Hohenstein on Schindler)

Bischof Günter. *Quiet Invaders Revisited: Biographies of Twentieth Century Immigrants to the United States* (TRANSATLANTICA 11). Innsbruck: StudienVerlag 2017 (with Katharina Prager on Viertel, Vera Kropf on Ilse Lichtblau Jahn, and Harmut Kroens on Eisler), 103-28, 223-30

-------. "American Bucks and Austrian Buccaneers: Sun Valley – The Making of America's First Winter Resort," in: Philipp Strobl/ Aneta Podkalicka, eds., *Leisure Culture and the Making of Modern Ski Resorts; A Transcultural Account* (Global Culture and Sports Series). London: Palgrave Macmillan, 2018

Carroll John, "30-year Gilead R&D vet Norbert Bischofberger is taking over as staffer #5 at an upstart biotech – and he's loving it," *Endpoints News,* May 24, 2018 https://endpts.com/30-year-gilead-rd-vet-norbert-bischofberger-is-starting-over-as-staffer-5-at-an-upstart-biotech-and-hes-loving-it/

Coleman Annie Gilbert. *Ski Style: Sport and Culture in the Rockies.* (CultureAmerica) Lawrence: University Press of Kansas 2014.

Coser Lewis. *Refugee Scholars in America: Their Impact and Their Experiences.* New Haven: Yale UP, 198

Daniels Roger. *Coming to America: A History of Immigration and Ethnicity in American Life.* 2nd ed. New York: Perennial 2002

Fleck Christian. *Etablierung in der Fremde: Vertriebene Wissenschaftler in den USA nach 1933.* Frankfurt: Campus Verlag, 2015

Gidl Anneliese/ Ian Scully. *"Let's ski, follow me!": Austrian Ski Pioneers in America.* [unpublished manuscript in possession of author]

Gutenbrunner Kurt. https://www.starchefs.com/cook/chefs/bio/kurt-gutenbrunner (accessed May 2, 2018)

Heilbut Anthony. *Exiled in Paradise: German Refugee Artists and Intellectuals in America from the 1930s to the Present.* Boston: Beacon Press 1983

Pelinka Anton. "The Impact of American Scholarship on Austrian Political Science: The Making of a Discipline." In: Günter Bischof/Anton Pelinka, eds., *The Americanization/ Westernization of Austria* (CAS 12). New Brunswick, NJ: Transaction 2004, 226-34

Piotrowska Anna G. "'Vienna Touch" in Hollywood: Viennese-Born/Educated Composers and Early Film Scores," in Joshua Parker/Ralph Poole, eds., *Austria and America: Cross Cultural Encounters 1865-1933* (American Studies in Austria 14). Vienna: LIT Verlag 2014, 95-108

Puck Wolfgang. http://wolfgangpuck.com/ (accessed May 2, 2018)

----. *Wolfgang Puck Makes It Easy: A Step-By-Step Collection for the Home Cook.* Nashville, TN: Thomas Nelson, 2004

Steiner Julian. "Thomas Ferlesch, Werkstatt Brooklyn, NY," Austrian Information 69 (Fall 2016): 63

Traussnig Florian. *Militärischer Widerstand von Aussen: Österreicher in der US-Armee und Kriegsgeheimdienst im Zweiten Weltkrieg.* Vienna: Böhlau 2015.

Ulrich Rudolf. *Österreicher in Hollywood: Ihr Beitrag zur Entwicklung des amerikanischen Films.* Vienna: Österreichische Staatsdruckerei,1993

US Department of Homeland Security/Office of Immigration Statistics, ed. *2008 Yearbook of Immigration Statistics.* Washington, DC 2009

Wasserman Janek. *The Marginal Revolutionaries: Austrian Economics from Coffeehouse to Tea Party.*[New Haven: Yale UP 2018 forthcoming]

CHAPTER 6

Bischof Günter/ Stefan Karner/ Barbara Stelzl-Marx, eds. *The Vienna Summit and Its Importance in International History.* Lanham: Lexington Books, 2014

-------/Ferdinand Karlhofer, eds. *Austrian International Position after the End of the Cold War* (CAS 22). New Orleans-Innsbruck: UNO Press-Innsbruck UP 2013 (Essays by Günter Bischof, Urusla Plassnik, Emil Brix, James Sheehan and Arnold Suppan)

-------/Fritz Plasser, eds. *The Schüssel Era in Austria* (CAS 18). New Orleans-Innsbruck: UNO Press-Innsbruck UP 2010

-------/Martin Kofler. "Austria's Postwar Occupation, the Marshall Plan, and Secret Rearmament as 'Westernizing Agents', 1945-1968." In: Günter Bischof/Anton Pelinka, eds. *The Americanization/Westernization of Austria* (CAS 12). New Brunswick, NJ: Transaction, 2003, 199-225

Gilde Benjamin. *Österreich im KSZE-Prozess 1969-1983: Neutraler Vermittler.* Munich: Oldenbourg Verlag 2013

Graf Maximilian/Sarah Knoll. "In transit or Asylum Seekers? Austria and the Cold War Refugees from the Communist Bloc." In: Günter Bischof/Dirk Rupnow, eds., *Migration in Austria* (CAS 26). New Orleans-Innsbruck: UNO Press-Innsbruck UP 2017, 91-112

Grunwald Henry. *One Man's America: A Journalist's Search for the Heart of His Country.* New York: Doubleday 1997

Kazanjian Dodie. Meet Max Hollein, the Metropolitan Museum's New Director. In: *Vogue*, Aug. 15, 2018 https://www.vogue.com/article/max-hollein-metropolitan-museum-director-interview-vogue-september-2018

Keene Brandon. "A Crusade against the 'Cowboy'? Austrian Anti-Americanism during the Presidency of George W. Bush, 2001-2009." MA thesis University of New Orleans 2015

Petritsch, Wolfgang. "Recent Balkans Diplomacy from an Austrian Perspective." In: Günter Bischof/Anton Pelinka/Michael Gehler, eds. *Austrian Foreign Policy in Historical Context* (CAS 14). New Brunswick, NJ: Transaction, 2006, 264-79

Rathkolb Oliver. "Austria's 'Ostpolitik' in the 1950s and 1960s: Honest Broker or Double Agent." In: *Austrian History Yearbook 26* (1995): 129-45

Reiter Margit/ Helga Embacher, eds. *Europa und der 11. September 2001.* Vienna: Böhlau 2011

Thun-Hohenstein Christoph. "Landmark Architecture as Cultural Hubs: The Schindler House in L.A. and the Austrian Cultural Forum," *Austrian Information* (Fall 2016): 27-29

Waldner Wolfgang. "Manhattan's Austrian Landmark," *Austrian Information* (Fall 2016): 30-33

Hollein Max, e-mail to the Met Membership, Aug. 15, 2018

Annual trade figures are in https://www.census.gov/foreign-trade/balance/c4330.htmlhttp://www.austria.org/trade-relations-today/

Trade groups, see https://diepresse.com/home/wirtschaft/5384928/Red-Bull-Glock-und-KTM-Oesterreichs-Aussenhandel-mit-den-USA#slide-5384928-0

Austrian business in the U.S., see http://www.advantageaustria.org/us/Oesterreich-in-den-USA.en.html

Individual businesses, see https://www.alpla.com/en; https://www.grassusa.com/; http://www.rosenbaueramerica.com/; https://www.palfinger.com/en-US/usa (all these websites accessed May 2/3, 2018)

Günter Bischof

Günter Bischof was educated in Austria and the United States. He received his PhD in American History from Harvard University. He is the Marshall Plan Professor of History at the University of New Orleans and the Director of its Austrian Marshall Plan Center for European Studies. He has published in the history of World War II and the Cold War, and more specifically on U.S. – Austrian relations and Austrian immigration to the U.S. in the 20th century.

Hannes Richter

Hannes Richter is a political scientist with the Austrian Embassy's Press and Information Service in the United States, where he focuses on political communication, public diplomacy, and nation brand. Trained in Austria and the United States, he received his PhD from the University of New Orleans, where he is also a Senior Research Fellow with the Austrian Marshall Plan Center for European Studies.

Biography

Photo Credits